TransFormative
Assessment
in Action

SUSTAINABLE
FORESTRY
INITIATIVE

Certified Fiber Sourcing
www.sfiprogram.org

Transformative Assessment in Action

An Inside Look at Applying the Process

W. JAMES
POPHAM

Alexandria, Virginia USA

1703 N. Beauregard St. • Alexandria, VA 22311-1714 USA
Phone: 800-933-2723 or 703-578-9600 • Fax: 703-575-5400
Website: www.ascd.org • E-mail: member@ascd.org
Author guidelines: www.ascd.org/write

Gene R. Carter, *Executive Director;* Judy Zimny, *Chief Program Development Officer;* Nancy Modrak, *Publisher;* Scott Willis, *Director, Book Acquisitions & Development;* Julie Houtz, *Director, Book Editing & Production;* Katie Martin, *Editor;* Georgia Park, *Senior Graphic Designer;* Mike Kalyan, *Production Manager;* Keith Demmons, *Desktop Publishing Specialist;* Kyle Steichen, *Production Specialist*

© 2011 by ASCD. All rights reserved. No part of this publication may be reproduced or transmitted in any form or by any means, electronic or mechanical, including photocopy, recording, or any information storage and retrieval system, without permission from ASCD. Readers who wish to duplicate material copyrighted by ASCD may do so for a small fee by contacting the Copyright Clearance Center (CCC), 222 Rosewood Dr., Danvers, MA 01923, USA (phone: 978-750-8400; fax: 978-646-8600; web: www.copyright.com). For requests to reprint rather than photocopy, contact ASCD's permissions office: 703-575-5749 or permissions@ascd.org. Translation inquiries: translations@ascd.org.

Printed in the United States of America. Cover art © 2011 by ASCD. ASCD publications present a variety of viewpoints. The views expressed or implied in this book should not be interpreted as official positions of the Association.

All web links in this book are correct as of the publication date below but may have become inactive or otherwise modified since that time. If you notice a deactivated or changed link, please e-mail books@ascd.org with the words "Link Update" in the subject line. In your message, please specify the web link, the book title, and the page number on which the link appears.

PAPERBACK ISBN: 978-1-4166-1124-0   ASCD product # 111008   n3/11
Also available as an e-book (see Books in Print for the ISBNs).

Quantity discounts for the paperback edition only: 10–49 copies, 10%; 50+ copies, 15%; for 1,000 or more copies, call 800-933-2723, ext. 5634, or 703-575-5634. For desk copies: member@ascd. org.

Library of Congress Cataloging-in-Publication Data

Popham, W. James.
 Transformative assessment in action : an inside look at applying the process / W. James Popham.
   p. cm.
 Includes bibliographical references and index.
 ISBN 978-1-4166-1124-0 (pbk. : alk. paper) 1. Educational tests and measurements. 2. School improvement programs. I. Title.
 LB3051.P614475 2011
 371.26--dc22
                          2010046205

22 21 20 19 18 17 16 15 14 13 12 11   1 2 3 4 5 6 7 8 9 10 11 12

In Memoriam

Lorraine Sprout
1951–2010

A teacher of 28 years who contributed
an essay to this book

Transformative Assessment in Action

An Inside Look at Applying the Process

Acknowledgments

Unlike the sometimes elusive authorial intent, authorial appreciation is far easier to identify. Writers usually supply readers with some up-front sentences thanking the people they ought to be thanking. I shall follow the tradition here and express my appreciation to several individuals who helped make this book a reality.

For openers, I appreciate the efforts of ASCD's book acquisition cabal. From my initial suggestion that a sequel to the ASCD book *Transformative Assessment* might entice more educators to tread the trail of formative assessment, Scott Willis, Carolyn Pool, and Genny Ostertag supplied consistent and remarkably supportive guidance. Early on, they admonished me to make sure that this book would be a "better than equal sequel," and they did their share to help make it so.

The ASCD editor who worked directly on this book gets my lasting thanks. Katie Martin has served as the chief editor for all five books that I have written for ASCD. Talk about a writer's getting lucky! Some editors only fuss with words and syntax. Katie gets inside the substance of a book and, given her considerable talent, smoothes out not only the rough edges of sentences, but also the wrinkles in a writer's thinking.

I am truly thankful to the many teachers (and the couple of administrators) who supplied the comments and testimonials you will find in Chapter 9. These educators are busy folks. Yet, without recompense (other than a gratis copy of a grateful author's book), they took time to explain the benefits formative assessment has brought to them and to their students, and why they think teachers should use formative assessment. Margaret Heritage, Caroline Wiley, Sara Bryant, Marnie Thompson, and Kathy Dyer helped me find these ace formative assessors. These five friends and colleagues get an $A+$ for the caliber of their nominations, and they get gobs of appreciation from me.

Finally, I want to thank my friend and word-processing wizard, Dolly Bulquerin, who cobbled together my separate chapters into a form that the ASCD folks would regard as an acceptable manuscript.

Thanks, really, to all of these people. I hope the book makes their efforts worthwhile.

WJP
2011

Introduction (and Reprise)

Not too long ago, I wrote a book about formative assessment (Popham, 2008). In that book's first paragraph, I said I would be describing a kind of classroom assessment intended to "fundamentally transform the way a teacher teaches" (p. vii), and as a consequence, the book's publisher gave it the title of *Transformative Assessment*. This book, the book you've just started to read, is a sequel to that earlier volume. In an effort to reduce confusion, I will refer to the earlier book as *"TA1"* and to this sequel as *"TA2."*

Why a Sequel?

I've never written a sequel before. Oh, I've certainly revised books, especially textbooks, so that my publishers could sell updated versions of the books to those who want "the latest word." But those revised editions aren't really sequels; they are updated, yet structurally similar, versions of an already written book. In contrast, *TA2* is a brand new book, with a mission that's different from that of its elder sibling. Let me explain.

As *Transformative Assessment* made its way into educators' hands, I found myself invited to make presentations and to direct workshops focused on how formative assessment could enhance teachers' effectiveness and improve students' learning. I was delighted to accept these invitations and, in 2009, I ended up making many such presentations throughout the United States, elaborating on the mission and content of *TA1* and spelling out what formative assessment is, what it isn't, how it is supported by solid research evidence, and the ways in which teachers could be encouraged to start using it.

These sorts of professional development sessions afford great opportunities to get acquainted with one's colleagues, and I established e-mail communication with educators from many of those sessions, especially with the school leaders who had set up my presentations. At first, I picked up some useful insights about the way formative assessment was being accepted in these schools. But, as time went by, what I began finding out from those e-mail communications was troubling.

"Yes," my school-leader correspondents told me, "the teachers you met at our sessions were and still are quite supportive of formative assessment. But relatively few of our teachers are actually using formative assessment in their own classrooms." According to my contacts, the most prevalent obstacle to getting teachers to use formative assessment was *insufficient professional development time*. Teachers didn't feel they had the time they needed to consider procedures and issues associated with formative assessment. Right behind the obstacle of insufficient professional development time, though, was a desperate need for *models of formative assessment in action*.

The Majesty of Modeling

For more than a year now, I've been polling local educators to get a better fix on what sorts of "examples" of formative assessment they want—what kinds of models would be most useful in getting them and their colleagues to give the formative assessment process a try. Most replied that they wanted videos of classrooms in which teachers and students were using formative assessment. And although I appreciated their suggestions, I think that what those educators were asking for isn't what they really need.

Perhaps you already know that formative assessment is *a planned process in which teachers or students use assessment-elicited evidence to improve what they're doing.* It calls for teachers and, in some instances, students to make a host of decisions. And because formative assessment is primarily about decisions, what is *most important* about it is not what goes on inside a classroom and can be captured by a camera crew, but *what goes on inside a teacher's head* and *inside students' heads.* We might be able to catch on video what it looks like for a teacher to gather assessment evidence that will be used in the formative assessment process. But for that video to be truly helpful as a model, it would need to play with a simultaneous voice-over track—something like the director's commentaries you find on DVDs—in which the teacher would explain the rationale for collecting this evidence at this particular time as well as the subsequent decisions about an instructional adjustment that the evidence informed.

I expect this kind of high-quality video professional development tool will be available one day. But I didn't want to wait. Every day that formative assessment is not used in a teacher's classroom is a day that students are not being taught as well as they could be—as well as they *should* be. So I decided to write a book that would take a reader "inside a teacher's head" as that teacher got ready for and implemented the formative assessment process. My paper-and-ink modeling may not be as vivid as a DVD with a director's commentary, and it's neither high-def nor 3–D, but I think it does what I set out to do: depict what goes on in the mind of a teacher who is employing formative assessment.

What's on the Menu

This book covers both the foundation of formative assessment and its applications. As you might guess, the foundation comes first.

In Chapter 1, I provide a new framework intended to give educators a firmer grasp on the various applications of the formative assessment process. I've done a heap of thinking about such an easy-to-understand framework, and those thoughts have been informed by literally hundreds of interactions with teachers and administrators throughout the United States. This framework might not be needed by all educators, but it surely helped me think more clearly about the most appropriate moments to employ the formative assessment process. I hope it helps you, too.

Chapter 2 takes a closer look at what I believe to be the blueprint for effective formative assessment—the learning progression—and prompts teachers to uncover the learning progressions that may already be present within their unit plans.

Then, it's on to formative assessment's applications and my own illustrations. In Chapters 3 through 8, we will first look at the various decisions—or *choice-points*—involved in planning various applications of formative assessment and then go inside some classrooms to focus on particular ways that teachers are using these applications. Immediately after the depictions of the classroom goings-on, you will read an interview with the classroom teacher whom you (and the interviewer) have just seen in action. This teacher comments on what he or she was thinking, planning, or deciding at key points of the formative assessment process. At the close of each chapter's interview, I isolate the chief insights I hope you will have snared from the interviews.

The obvious question: Who are these teachers we'll be seeing in action—these teachers who will be giving us an inside look at the process of formative assessment? They are amalgams, each an imagined combination based on what I've learned from (1) teachers who successfully use formative assessment, (2) supervisors who have observed and discussed formative assessment with teachers who use it, and (3) what the research evidence suggests is a sensible way for a formatively assessing teacher to behave in such situations. These teachers are not written as never-make-an-error pedagogical paragons but, rather, as professionals who look to their own experiences or the results of relevant research and arrive at instructional decisions they believe make sense for the kids they teach.

Happily, one of the most consoling findings of formative assessment research is that teachers do not need to carry out formative assessment in a single, prescribed manner. The teachers in these interviews are meant to be savvy educators who have tried certain approaches, have sometimes stumbled, and yet have arrived at what are, for them, viable ways to use the formative assessment process. As you "see" them in action, read their interview comments, and read my follow-up commentary on their comments, I hope that you will think about how you, as a teacher yourself or as a school leader working with teachers, would approach the same decisions they encounter.

Because I knew I wanted to use a series of fictional teachers to illustrate various applications of formative assessment in this book, I immediately invited contributions from *real* teachers, identified by friends and colleagues as top-flight users of formative assessment —the very same sorts of educators I hoped to conjure in my amalgamations. I was delighted with the number of them who agreed to submit commentaries for inclusion in the book. In these commentaries, which you'll find in Chapter 9, they describe why they use formative assessment and, in several cases, *how* they go about making important formative assessment decisions.

Finally, after we have squeezed all the insights out of our teachers, real and fictional, we'll close the book with some next-step actions for educators who want to see formative assessment used more widely.

At the end of every chapter, you'll find a set of reflection questions intended to extend your thinking about the chapter's content. In some instances, you'll be asked to reflect on particular formative assessment activities or, possibly, on choices that are almost certain to confront users of formative assessment. Hopefully, these questions will serve as discussion catalysts for those reading the book as part of professional study.

Well, this is what's coming in *TA2*. Before we get to that, though, let's look quickly at what went on in *TA1*.

Reprise, or a Substantially Squeezed Summary of *TA1*'s Most Important Content

If you've already read *TA1*, preferably with such fevered intensity that you committed enormous portions of that book to memory, then what's in the rest of this Introduction will pretty familiar—a refresher, let us say. If, however, you have not read *TA1*, and can deal with the shame of such a shortcoming, the following recapitulation will ready you for the upcoming chapters in this book.

A Key Definition

In my 2008 book *Transformative Assessment*, I offered this definition of formative assessment:

> Formative assessment is a planned process in which assessment-elicited evidence of students' status is used by teachers to adjust their ongoing instructional procedures or by students to adjust their current learning tactics. (p. 6)

If I had to choose the single, most important thing I hope readers would have learned from *TA1*, it would be this definition, stressing that formative assessment is a *process*, not a test, and a process that's carefully *planned.* In this process, *assessments*, both formal and informal, supply the evidence about "where students currently are" so that teachers and students can figure out how to reduce the gap between where students currently are and where those students should be when instruction wraps up.

Formative assessment is *not* a collection of "interim tests" administered periodically to all students in a school or district. Such interim tests may be called "formative," but labeling them as such does not automatically make those tests what commercial vendors have chosen to call them. Nor is formative assessment what takes place when teachers make an instructional adjustment in response to "sensing" student confusion or by inferring it, based on a classroom full of puzzled faces or abuzz with atypical murmuring.

Yes, after an apparent instructional misfire, a sensible teacher will regroup and try another sort of explanation. That's good teaching, and it's something that all teachers should do. But it is not formative assessment—because there's been no planning, no assessment-elicited evidence, and no prior thought on the teacher's part about what sort of instructional adjustments might work to set the lesson to rights. Being responsive to students' reactions makes all sorts of pedagogical sense, but teachers who point to this kind of sound practice as proof that they are "already doing formative assessment" are mistaken.

Note also that, according to this definition, the formative assessment process can be used *either* by teachers to alter their instructional activities or by students to spruce up their learning tactics. It can also be used by both teachers and students at the same time.

Research Ratification

Teachers and students paying attention to the assessed consequences of instruction and taking action upon them makes gallons of good sense without any research support whatsoever. Happily, we have it anyway. As I noted in *TA1*, the most compelling collection of relevant empirical research supporting formative assessment is found in the review of classroom assessment investigations by two British researchers, Paul Black and Dylan Wiliam (1998). Starting with about 10 years' worth of published research studies dealing with classroom assessment, almost 700 studies in all, these two analysts selected the 250 strongest investigations, reviewed the findings pertinent to instructionally oriented use of classroom assessments, and then drew the following conclusion:

> The research reported here shows conclusively that formative assessment does improve learning. (Black and Wiliam, 1998, p. 61)

Moreover, Black and Wiliam concluded that the student gains in learning triggered by formative assessment were "amongst the largest ever reported for educational interventions" (p. 61) and that "we have not come across any report of negative effects following an enhancement of formative practice" (p. 17). Finally, these two researchers affirmed the robustness of the formative assessment process by asserting that "Significant gains can be achieved by many different routes, and initiatives here are not likely to fail through neglect of delicate and subtle features" (p. 61).

It is difficult for anyone to spend much time with the influential Black and Wiliam review of classroom assessment research without concluding that formative assessment works, it works big time, and its positive effect can be obtained in many ways, as long those employing it incorporate the process's central attributes.

Thinking in Levels

In my exploration of formative assessment in *TA1*, I broke it down into the following four "levels":

• *Level 1: Teachers' Instructional Adjustments,* wherein teachers collect assessment evidence and use it to decide whether to adjust their current or immediately upcoming instruction in order to improve its effectiveness.

• *Level 2: Students' Learning Tactic Adjustments,* in which students rely on assessment evidence regarding their current skills/knowledge status to decide whether to adjust the procedures they use when trying to learn something.

• *Level 3: Classroom Climate Shift,* whereby an attempt is made to bring about a fundamental change in the teacher's and students' (1) learning expectations, (2) perceptions about who is responsible for students' learning, and (3) attitude about the role of classroom assessment.

• *Level 4: Schoolwide Implementation,* in which an entire school or a district adopts one or more levels of formative assessment, typically via professional development or the use of professional learning communities (PLCs).

In retrospect, it would have been better for me to have described these four variations of formative assessment as "types" or "categories" rather than as levels, because it's not strictly necessary to implement them in numerical order, that is, to use Level 1, then Level 2, and so on. A school's leaders might decide to initially adopt only Level 1 formative assessment (teachers' instructional adjustments), then move directly to Level 4 formative assessment (schoolwide implementation) without necessarily first trying to install either Level 2 or Level 3.

What does installing these categories of formative assessment entail? Well, in *TA1*, I identify several suggested steps. You'll see them depicted in Figure A, and you can read more about these steps in the pages of that book.

FIGURE A

Transformative Assessment's Suggested Steps for Establishing Formative Assessment

Level 1: Teachers' Instructional Adjustments
1. Identify adjustment occasions.
2. Select assessments.
3. Establish adjustment triggers.
4. Make instructional adjustments.

Level 2: Students' Learning Tactic Adjustments
1. Consider adjustment occasions.
2. Consider assessments.
3. Consider adjustment triggers.
4. Consider adjusting learning tactics.

Level 3: Classroom Climate Shifts
1. Distribute classroom climate guidelines.
2. Seek trust constantly and nurture it seriously.
3. Model and reinforce appropriate conduct.
4. Solicit students' advice on classroom climate.
5. Assess students' relevant affective status.

Level 4: Schoolwide Implementation
1. Establish professional development to support formative assessment.
2. Establish professional learning communities focused on the implementation and refinement of formative assessment.

Learning Progressions as the Process Foundation

In *TA1*, I explained that a *learning progression* is a sequenced set of subskills and bodies of knowledge (*building blocks*) a teacher believes students must master en route to mastering a demanding cognitive skill of significant curricular importance (a *target curricular aim*). To put it another way, a learning progression is a formal, thought-through outline of the *key content of instruction*—what's pivotal to be taught and mastered, and in what sequence. As such, it's a foundation for sound instruction and effective planning. It's also the backbone of a sensible, *planned* approach to formative assessment.

As I look back at *TA1*, though, I fear I may have made learning progressions too fear-inducing. Yes, coming up with superb learning progressions can be a really challenging task for teachers. But to make the formative assessment process purr, it is not necessary that every learning progression be "superb." In this book, I'll offer some suggestions about how teachers can draw on available curricular and instructional materials to come up with suitably serviceable learning progressions. Sure it's tough to think through the components of a learning progression. But any teacher can do it.

Thematic Threads

One of my missions is to help educators see formative assessment as something that is both worth doing and *eminently doable.* Of course, many of today's teachers, with considerable justification, have become negatively disposed toward anything even remotely related to testing. Such teachers think there's far too much testing going on, its consequences are way too serious, and it gobbles up too much teaching time. As an antidote to this sort of anti-test thinking, I want to reiterate a persistent theme from *TA1:* Formative assessment is more about teaching than it is about testing. At bottom, it is an *instruction-enhancing* process. It really is.

All right, now that we have taken a terse, over-the-shoulder look back at *TA1*, it's time to turn our attention to how the formative assessment process can be applied. As the title of this sequel suggests, *TA2* is focused on the application of formative assessment. Chapter 1, then, lays out a framework for educators who want to think about ways to turn formative assessment talk into formative assessment action.

1

Applying the Formative
Assessment Process

A *process*, according to my dictionary, is "a systematic series of actions directed to some end." Such a definition fits formative assessment to a tee, for it accurately depicts the carefully planned steps involved when teachers or students use assessment-elicited evidence to make adjustments in what they are doing to teach or to learn. The "some end," in this case, is always an enhancement of students' learning.

Another feature of a process is that it can be applied in many situations. For example, back when I was a graduate research assistant pursuing a doctorate at Indiana University, my professors directed me to study various "electronic troubleshooting techniques" used by the U.S. Air Force during World War II. These were techniques employed to train maintenance personnel to accurately identify malfunctioning components in electronic equipment, such as radar systems and navigation instruments. My professors thought that some of these troubleshooting techniques might be applicable to teaching children how to solve complex mathematical problems and sent me off to conduct the research. One of the troubleshooting techniques I kept running into was something called the "Half-Split Process." It directed all maintenance personnel to split a malfunctioning system in half, choose one of those halves, and look there for the malfunctioning component. If everything in the selected half of the system turned out to have no problem in it, the technician's search would shift to the other half of the system. That half would be split in two, and the whole cycle would began again. By repeatedly "half-splitting" sections of a malfunctioning system into smaller and smaller units, the maintenance person was almost always able to winnow the search and identify the offending component. It worked when maintenance workers needed to repair electronic hardware, hydraulic systems, or any kind of complex equipment in which defective components were causing trouble.

A properly conceptualized process can be applied in myriad situations and to address a variety of challenges. Formative assessment is just such a process. What we're going to look at in this chapter are the ways in which formative assessment can be used.

The Applications of Formative Assessment

As we know, the formative assessment process involves the gathering and analysis of assessment-elicited evidence for the purpose of determining when and how to adjust instructional activities or learning tactics in order to achieve learning goals.

This chapter, organized around those potential adjustments, will supply you with an *application framework*—that is, a framework to help you determine when the formative assessment process might be profitably applied. And, of course, "profitably applied" in this instance is synonymous with "used to enhance kids' learning." There are five potential applications of formative assessment:

1. To make an immediate instructional adjustment
2. To make a near-future instructional adjustment
3. To make a last-chance instructional adjustment
4. To make a learning tactic adjustment
5. To promote a classroom climate shift

As teachers consider installing the formative assessment process in their own classrooms, one of the most significant choices will be determining *which* formative assessment application to employ.

That's because breaking them out in this way helps ensure thorough planning, proper preparation, and ultimate success.

Application 1: For Immediate Instructional Adjustments

Using formative assessment to make an immediate instructional adjustment means the teacher gathers data, analyzes it, and decides whether or not to change instruction right then, in that class session, in that moment. Immediate instructional adjustments can be based either on (1) teacher-administered assessment procedures, such as brief quizzes, or (2) student-reported levels of understanding.

Consider this scenario. Ms. Lee's 8th grade English students are midway through the first week of a three-week unit on punctuation. In the middle of the class session, Ms. Lee posts several multiple-choice questions designed to measure students' understanding of the day's lesson, which focuses on distinguishing between situations calling for s-apostrophe (s') versus apostrophe-s ('s). This is a subskill they must acquire in order to achieve the overall unit objective.

Ms. Lee uses her laptop computer and projector to present the multiple-choice questions one at a time. At her signal, the students hold up letter-cards to signify which of the choice options they believe to be correct. Ms. Lee scans the cards, making mental notes to herself. What she sees suggests her students are very confused. The number and variety of incorrect responses suggest not only that they have not mastered the "s-apostrophe" subskill, but also that they have misinterpreted the role of the apostrophe in such instances. Ms. Lee had anticipated this possibility, as students in previous years' classes had stumbled in similar ways.

With her analysis complete and a conclusion reached, Ms. Lee makes an immediate instructional adjustment. Rather than spend the second half of the class tackling the use of colons and semicolons, as she'd originally planned, she launches into a new instructional activity. First she tries to re-explain how apostrophes can make nouns possessive, but must be placed before or after the noun's final s, depending on whether the noun is singular or plural. She then distributes a 10-item practice sheet calling for students to distinguish between proper and improper uses of an apostrophe-*s* and an *s*-apostrophe. She models—step by step—how to respond to the first two practice items, and then asks the students to work with their pre-assigned study-pair partner to complete the remaining items. When they finish, she explains, they should pick up a copy of a prepared answer key, which provides brief explanations for all 10 practice items. Study-pairs are to compare the key's answers and explanations to their own in an effort to clarify any misunderstandings.

The virtue of immediate instructional adjustment is that it allows teachers to diagnose, address, and correct students' misconceptions instead of letting those misconceptions ferment overnight, after which they can be far more difficult to expunge. But while this is a clearly useful application of formative assessment, it definitely calls for advance work on the part of the teacher to predict what might go amiss in students' understanding and then to prepare suitable instructional responses.

Application 2: For Near-Future Instructional Adjustments

Applying the formative assessment process to make a *near-future instructional adjustment* involves the teacher's collecting assessment evidence of students' status relative to a longer-term instructional aim for the purpose of informing decisions about what to do better or differently in the next few class sessions.

Suppose Mr. Collins is in the midst of a six-week social studies unit designed to teach students to become skilled in analyzing political candidates' arguments. He has created a *learning progression* containing three subordinate subskills, each of which he believes is crucial to developing the overall analytic skill: (1) determining whether a political candidate's argument employs factual or distorted information, (2) identifying whether a candidate has or hasn't committed any logical reasoning errors, and (3) identifying the extent to which a candidate has relied on objective versus inflammatory language while presenting an argument.

One Tuesday, at about the four-week mark of this six-week unit, Mr. Collins asks students to complete an in-class, not-to-be-graded set of exercises based on applying the unit's second subskill, Logical Reasoning. That evening, he reviews the completed exercises and discovers that about half of the class seems to be seriously at sea. Mr. Collins is surprised by this worse-than-foreseen performance and decides that ameliorative action is warranted. He sees that his students seem confused by several sorts of logical fallacies, such as the difference between correlation and causation. He intends to re-explain each of these logical errors and illustrate them with examples that his students will readily understand. He also prepares a follow-up set of five take-home practice exercises dealing exclusively with the Logical Reasoning subskill.

Wednesday's lesson, focusing on Inflammatory Language (the third subskill in his learning progression) goes on as planned, but that Thursday, two days after the original collection of evidence, Mr. Collins supplies the new explanation of Logical Reasoning. He asks those students whose performance on the exercises indicated they were well on their way to mastering this subskill to serve as short-term peer tutors, and then sets aside 30 minutes for student-to-student tutorials. Mr. Collins also distributes the take-home practice exercises (along with an answer key) so that all students can apply their growing mastery of the Logical Reasoning subskill. He doesn't grade these exercises, but he does review students' responses to see if additional near-future instructional adjustments will be necessary. As is always the case with the formative assessment process, he will have done at least some preliminary thinking about what sorts of instructional actions might be taken if the data suggest the need for further instructional alterations. With the evidence in, Mr. Collins has time for additional analyses, can think through potential instructional options in light of the data's particulars, and can fine-tune his adjustment plans accordingly.

Application 3: For Last-Chance Instructional Adjustments

In the waning hours of a planned instructional sequence, when a teacher wants to discover whether students have mastered the target curricular aim they have been working toward, that teacher may apply formative assessment for the purpose of *last-chance instructional adjustments.* Instructional time still remains, and if the assessment evidence suggests that students are not at mastery or close to it, the teacher can provide additional or different instruction designed to get students back on track before the unit's scheduled conclusion—and before the unit's summative assessment.

This application of the formative assessment is often associated not just with the ends of units but also with the approach of an accountability test, particularly when teachers have a reasonably clear idea of what that test will cover. As an example, think about an annual statewide language arts exam that requires 8th grade students write (1) an original persuasive essay and (2) an appropriate 100-word summary of a 1,000-word magazine article. If too many students in a given school fail to perform satisfactorily on one or both of these tasks, the school will face serious penalties. With the date of this high-stakes test approaching, all the 8th grade teachers in a school agree to apply formative assessment to make last-chance instructional adjustments. They create a brand-new, essentially parallel form of the state's language arts accountability test—a "dress-rehearsal exam," which they administer three weeks before the "real" state test date. They score students' responses on both the persuasive essay and the written summary. Then, depending on their students' performances, certain teachers decide to spend the remaining classroom instructional hours dealing with those aspects of persuasive essay writing or article summarizing that appear to warrant additional instruction.

This application of formative assessment is appropriate for any genuinely important curricular outcome. But it's essential that a dress-rehearsal exam contain a sufficient number of items assessing the essential subskills and bodies of knowledge so a teacher can get a fairly accurate fix on where instructional support is required. Moreover, teachers needs to plan what they will do instructionally to address the mastery deficits uncovered by the dress-rehearsal exam before the subsequent real exam.

Application 4: For Learning Tactic Adjustments

The fourth way that formative assessment can be used is for the purpose of enabling students to use assessment evidence to monitor their own progress and decide whether they need to change the manner in which they're attempting to learn.

Students choose all kinds of ways to learn based on many factors, including personal preference, longtime habits, and the advice of past teachers. Some students may read teacher-assigned materials and complete homework activities without discussing this material with anyone, while others in the same class with the same assignments may discuss reading and homework at length with their family members and classmates. One 10th grader may prepare for a history test by reading through her notes three times with high-volume music slamming into her skull, while another 10th grader studies for the same test by translating his notes into an illustrated time line, working in tomblike silence.

Although this fourth application of formative assessment revolves around what students do, the teacher's role is significant. It's the teacher who establishes the expectation and the conditions so that each student can monitor his or her own learning progress and decide whether or not to make a learning tactic adjustment. To be completely candid, today's educators have few experiences to guide them in how to successfully install and nurture this application of the formative assessment process. The benefits of it, however, can be remarkable—namely, students who are actively reviewing their own classroom assessment data, connecting these outcomes to their own inputs, and making changes so that their efforts will yield more satisfactory results. Students engaged in learning tactic adjustment take an active role in their education, and this self-direction will surely serve them well in their future endeavors both inside and outside of school.

Application 5: For Promoting a Classroom Climate Change

The fifth and final application of the formative assessment process works to make a wholesale, teacher-led change in the "learning atmosphere" of a classroom, shifting that atmosphere from a traditional, often competitive orientation to a more learning-for-all orientation. Such a shift in classroom climate typically results from three significant changes:

1. *A change in learning expectations.* It is no longer assumed that substantial learning is only possible for well-motivated students who possess sufficient innate academic aptitude. The teacher and the students see substantial learning as likely for all students, irrespective of how "smart" any student happens to be.

2. *A change in the locus of responsibility for learning.* It is no longer assumed that the teacher is overwhelmingly responsible for students' learning. The teacher and students agree that students bear significant responsibility for their own learning and for the learning of their classmates.

3. *A change in the role of classroom assessment.* Classroom tests are no longer viewed as the means to make grade-determining comparisons among students or to motivate students to study harder. Instead, classroom assessments are seen by teachers as the means to gather evidence necessary to inform instructional adjustments and by students as the means to gather evidence to make learning tactic adjustments. The vast majority of classroom tests are not graded at all.

One way to think of this fifth application of formative assessment is to regard it as a *consummate implementation* of the process that will secure maximum instructional mileage. As you've seen, there are applications of formative assessment focused on teachers' assessment-based decisions about whether or not instructional

adjustments are appropriate. There's also an application of formative assessment focused on students' assessment-based decisions
about whether to adjust their learning tactics. Well, because this
fifth application of formative assessment promotes a complete shift
in classroom climate, it is necessary to employ at least one or more
teacher-focused and one or more student-focused applications of
formative assessment. Promoting the three significant changes in
classroom climate identified above requires a total, no-holds-barred
effort.

Five Applications, One Process

We've now considered five different ways that the formative assessment process can be applied in a classroom. For a graphic representation of the applications, see Figure 1.1. What's crucial for you to
recognize is that all five of these applications are dependent on the
same fundamental process.

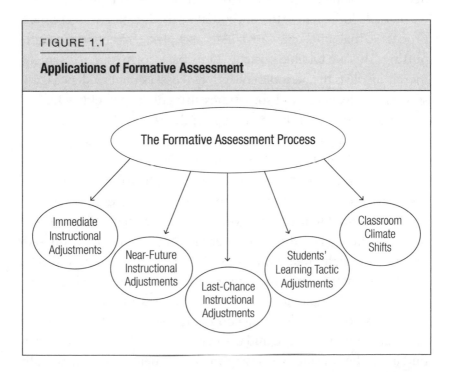

FIGURE 1.1

Applications of Formative Assessment

Much, although certainly not all, of a teacher's thinking about formative assessment occurs before any instruction actually takes place. As you'll see when we dig into each of these five applications of formative assessment, two factors typically turn out to be most instrumental in a teacher's planning. The first of these factors is linked to *when* an adjustment decision must be made and implemented: immediately or later? The second factor involves *the kind of assessment evidence that will be used,* which requires the teacher to decide what kinds of assessments to employ.

Some teachers who are on the fence about giving formative assessment a try might be fearful that it requires a "paragon of pedagogical prowess," that is, the ability to make myriad on-the-spot decisions about how to assess students and, thereafter, what sorts of adjustments to make. Well, although a number of pedagogical paragons can be found in our schools, you do not have to be such a teacher in order to implement formative assessment. All that's truly necessary is a modest amount of thoughtful, up-front planning. Yes, it's possible for teachers to conceptualize the formative assessment process so that it becomes amazingly complex, and hence, truly off-putting. This is a terrible mistake. At its base, formative assessment merely involves the periodic collection of assessment evidence from students so teachers and sometimes students can decide whether or not to adjust what they're doing. In the remainder of the book, you'll learn how to make plans so that this fundamentally simple process works well for you and your students.

As we take our closer look at each application of formative assessment in the chapters to come, you'll also see how fictional teachers attempt to use formative assessment in that manner. These teachers may go about things differently than you would yourself, but this is all right. Remember, current research evidence indicates that the formative assessment process is quite muscular; it can tolerate teachers' employing it in many variations and still work well.

In this book, I'm devoting comparatively little attention to the particular of how to build and use classroom assessments. You can find a number of suitable classroom assessment procedures, both formal and informal, in *TA1*. Additional particulars about how to construct and employ measurement devices and procedures are available in almost any textbook focused on classroom assessment (see, for example, Popham, 2011; Stiggins, 2006). However, it is worth emphasizing that measurement devices matter. To make formative assessment as successful as it can be, the assessment evidence on which it relies needs to be accurate. Formative assessment based on shabby assessment instruments and procedures is destined to become shabby formative assessment.

Reflection Questions

1. From the perspective of promoting wider use of formative assessment, what are the advantages and disadvantages of looking at formative assessment in component parts: as four levels (as was done in *TA1*) or as five applications (as is done in this book)?

2. If you had to come up with your own brief but accurate explanation of formative assessment—an explanation suitable for members of a non-educator audience—how would you describe it?

3. What are the similarities and differences in the five applications of formative assessment outlined in this chapter? Consider coming back to this question after you have finished reading the five chapters that explore each application in greater depth to see if your views have changed.

2

Learning Progressions: Blueprints for the Formative Assessment Process

You've seen that formative assessment is a process that can be applied in several ways, all of which depend on the collection of assessment evidence. Sometimes teachers collect this evidence through the use of fairly formal tests; sometimes the evidence comes from less formal assessment procedures.

It's important to stress, though, that formative assessment involves far more than a teacher's spontaneously tossing tons of tests at students or frequently calling for thumbs-up/thumbs-down agreement to the question, "Does everyone understand?" No, formative assessment is definitely a *planned* process, and the key component of this planning is unquestionably the *learning progression.* It is not an overstatement to assert that learning progressions are completely indispensable if the formative assessment process is to function properly. They provide the blueprint for the process—the structure for evidence gathering and adjustment occasions—and serve as a measure of assurance that the evidence-informed adjustments will improve student learning. If a ship without a rudder is, by definition, rudderless, then formative assessment without a learning progression often becomes plan-less.

Looking at Learning Progressions

I think the definition of "learning progression" I supplied in *TA1* is a good one:

> A learning progression is a sequenced set of subskills or bodies of enabling knowledge that, it is thought, students must master en route to mastering a more remote target curricular aim. (Popham, 2008, p. 24)

Laying out what a student needs to master en route to mastering a subsequent curricular aim requires clear thinking and the use of precise terminology. So let's define the key terms involved in the above definition. That's right; it's time for definitions within a definition!

• *Target curricular aim.* This is an important curricular goal being sought for students; it is preferably some sort of higher-level cognitive skill. Frequently, a target curricular aim is simply an objective for an extended-duration teaching unit, such as a three-week unit promoting students' mastery of an important skill in social studies. A target curricular aim might also be a key learning goal for an entire course.

• *Building block.* Each building block within a learning progression is either (1) a body of knowledge or (2) a subskill that the progression's architect believes students must master before they can conquer that learning progression's target curricular aim.

• *A body of enabling knowledge.* This term describes and attempts to circumscribe the nature of what students must know or understand in order to master a learning progression's target curriculum aim. A body of enabling knowledge might be a set of information, principles, or procedures.

• *A subskill.* This term describes what students must be able to do in order to master a learning progression's target curricular aim. In most instances, subskill building blocks identify a specific cognitive skill. If the target curricular aim happens to be psychomotor in nature, the subskills in the learning progression would typically also be of a psychomotor sort.

Put in colloquial language, a learning progression lays out the sequence of lesser stuff a student must learn in order to master subsequent, more significant stuff. Learning progressions are often depicted graphically, as you see in Figure 2.1.

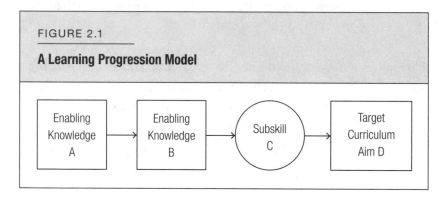

FIGURE 2.1

A Learning Progression Model

It is not necessary for knowledge-based building blocks to precede subskill-based building blocks, as they do in the figure, but in actual practice this often turns out to be the case. We'll talk more about sequencing shortly, but before we do, I want to address a critical and potentially confusing point: that the term "learning progression," even as it pertains to a sequenced set of subskills and bodies of enabling knowledge it is thought students must master en route to mastering a more remote target curricular aim, can be used to describe two substantially different things.

Two Conceptions, Both Useful

Currently, a number of first-rate scholars are attempting to build learning progressions to provide teachers with a better understanding of how students typically learn important things. Heritage (2008) provides an especially useful picture of the nature of these learning progressions when she concludes that they typically (1) describe how students' learning of particular things develops over a lengthy period of time, perhaps several years or more in duration;

(2) are focused on students' attainment of really important curricular outcomes such as the "big ideas" in a content area; and (3) are research-confirmed in the sense that serious empirical studies have been carried out to demonstrate a learning progression's building blocks—initially derived analytically—are both necessary and properly ordered.

To illustrate the kinds of formal inquiry that might be needed to confirm such a learning progression's quality, we might find researchers rounding up one group of students who had mastered a particular building block and a second group of students who had not. An experiment would then be carried out to see if, based on their subsequent mastery of a more remote curricular aim, those students who had mastered this particular building block were more successful than those students who hadn't. Other experiments might track how variations in building-block sequence affect rates of remote-aim mastery.

The kinds of learning progressions emerging from this approach could be described as long-duration, research-ratified, and focused on high-import outcomes. Their creation is exacting, time-consuming, and costly. (Just imagine how much research activity is necessary to *demonstrate* that most students learn things optimally in a particular order.) For descriptive convenience, I will hereafter refer to these as *uppercase learning progressions*. That is, considering the amount of energy required to create and sanctify one of these building-block sequences, I find myself thinking of them as being composed solely of capital letters: LEARNING PROGRESSIONS.

Would educators benefit from uppercase learning progressions? Absolutely! Could a teacher come up with better set of day-to-day instructional activities if that teacher had access to research-verified insights into the sequence in which most students learn the topic that the teacher is trying to teach? Again, absolutely. And this is why I hope that those researchers who are striving to create uppercase learning progressions will be sublimely successful. The more uppercase learning progressions teachers have at their disposal, the better job those teachers can do with their students.

Here's the catch, though. At the moment, there are relatively few uppercase learning progressions available, and it's likely to be a decade or two before this situation changes. That's about how long it will take for researchers to come up with enough long-duration, *research-confirmed* learning progressions focused on really important curricular aims.

But there are students to be taught in our classrooms *right now,* and what the teachers of those students need in order to make formative assessment flourish can be characterized as *lowercase learning progressions.* Lowercase learning progressions focus on instruction that requires between several weeks' worth of class time to a full semester or even an entire school year, if the target curricular aim is especially significant. They are based not on research investigations but on teachers' conceptual analyses and subsequent conclusions about which building blocks are necessary to master a target curriculum aim and the best way to sequence those building blocks. Because we're talking about informed best guesses here, not every learning progression a teacher creates will automatically be a winner, but most can be improved on the basis of trial-and-error usage in real classrooms with real kids.

Both uppercase and lowercase kinds of learning progressions can make a contribution to a teacher's decision making. But practically speaking, if you are reading this book, you are more likely to be working with lowercase learning progressions than with uppercase ones. So, from this point forward, when I use the label "learning progressions," I will be referring to *lowercase* learning progressions.

The Role of Learning Progressions in Formative Assessment

Learning progressions indicate to teachers *when* to collect the assessment evidence that undergirds the formative assessment process. Here's how this happens.

In order to master the target curricular aim for which the learning progression has been built, students must master each building block in that learning progression. And the way for a teacher to ensure that each building block is mastered is to assess its mastery and look at the assessment evidence so an instructional or learning tactic adjustment can be made if it's necessary. Simply put, linking formative assessment occasions to the building blocks in a learning progression is effective because it allows the teacher to be certain students are learning what they must learn. And, frankly, it's an extremely practical aid in planning. So for the teacher who wants to know, "When should I gather data for the purposes of formative assessment?" there's a simple answer: "At minimum, before you move on to the next building block in your learning progression." More specifically speaking, near the conclusion of whatever instruction is focused on that building block, leaving enough time in your lesson plans so that adjustments in instruction or learning tactics can have a positive effect on students' learning.

In addition to assessing and then making adjustment decisions about each building block, teachers can decide, based on personal preferences and individual classroom circumstances (such as a particular class's background knowledge), what *else* they might want to assess. That might be subcomponents of the building blocks or other topics teachers have worked into instruction that may not lead directly to mastery of the target curricular aim, yet enrich students' experiences.

In a moment, we'll be looking closer at the particulars of how to build a learning progression. As you read more about the process, you'll see that although the conceptual analyses to build these progressions can be carried out solo, there are advantages to teachers' joining forces for this effort.

Key Choice-Points When Building a Learning Progression

Teachers who set out to build a learning progression face five pivotal choice-points, listed in Figure 2.2. Let's look at each of them.

FIGURE 2.2
_____

Five Choice-Points for Building a Learning Progression

---

1. **Which curricular aims.** What curricular outcomes should be the targets of learning progressions?

2. **What the grain size of the building blocks should be.** How broad or how narrow should a learning progression's building blocks be?

3. **How many building blocks there should be.** For a particular target curricular aim, what is an optimal number of building blocks?

4. **Which building blocks.** What subskills or bodies of enabling knowledge should constitute a learning progression?

5. **How the building blocks should be sequenced.** What is the optimal order for a learning progression's building blocks?

Choice-Point 1: Which Curricular Aims Merit the Creation of a Learning Progression

This very first choice-point is really more fundamental than it may initially appear. Because teachers need to rely on a learning progression to make formative assessment function properly, decisions about which curricular targets a learning progression should be built for are, in fact, decisions about when to use formative assessment at all!

One practical way of addressing this issue would be for a teacher to prioritize the target curricular aims to be tackled during a semester/school year, then use formative assessment (complete with its necessary learning progressions) only for those aims that can be promoted *without formative assessment's becoming overwhelming.* It would be better for a teacher, year in and year out, to use formative assessment for only a few teaching units per year than to use it so often one year that, in years to come, formative assessment isn't used at all.

Building a learning progression takes time and effort, and it makes no sense to apply a potent-but-demanding process to promote students' mastery of minutiae. I advise reserving formative assessment and learning progression creation for curricular aims that are complex, cognitive skills. For example, a 5th grade teacher might create a learning progression aimed at getting students to master writing summaries of stories they have read, but might forgo one dealing with students' mastery of the semicolon. A geography teacher might create a learning progression aimed at getting students to create maps that accurately illustrate a locale's societally salient geographic variables, but skip it when dealing with lessons or units focused on students' memorizing information of the location of nations on a continent.

Knowledge-focused curricular aims, such as those calling for students to memorize sets of facts, conventions, or principles, are surely important, for such knowledge often serves as the springboard for higher-level skills incorporating this sort of knowledge. But if students are supposed to memorize and understand large lumps of knowledge, there is usually no need to employ any sort of learning progression. That's because the target curricular aim (the knowledge to be mastered) is, itself, what students are supposed to learn.

To help decide whether a target curricular aim is worthy of the formative assessment process and, of course, worthy of having its own learning progression, teachers might consider the following questions:

1. Is this target curricular aim a cognitive skill—and one that would take more than a class session or two to teach?

2. Will this skill be applicable in a wide range of subsequent situations, either in school or in the non-school world?

3. Is this skill a foundation for future learning either in this course or in courses students will be taking down the line?

4. Is mastery of this skill something that students must display on a subsequent high-stakes assessment of some sort?

5. Is this target curricular aim of such importance to students that it warrants a meaningful expenditure of my energy in properly implementing the formative assessment process?

Perhaps not all of these questions need to be answered in the affirmative before a target curricular aim is regarded as worthy of having a learning progression created for it. But two or three negative answers should make a teacher think twice, or thrice, before getting down to work of learning progression creation.

Choice-Point 2: What the "Grain Size" of the Building Blocks Will Be

Grain size describes the nature of a building block. It tells you how narrow or how broad a body of knowledge is, or how complex or demanding a subskill is. The "smaller" the grain of a progression's building block, the more building blocks there will be in that progression. Likewise, the "larger" the grain, the fewer building blocks that progression will contain.

As discussed, a teacher must collect assessment evidence for every building block in a learning progression. So teachers who build learning progressions with lots of small-grain building blocks need to plan, design, and administer more assessments; review and analyze more assessment evidence; and be prepared for more frequent instructional adjustments. Opting for fewer, larger-grain building blocks means fewer mandatory assessments, less review and analysis, and fewer occasions for adjustment. The "small-grain" approach has the potential to be more exact, but it is also more complicated and much more time-consuming. "Small-grainers" are at risk for setting for themselves an assessment task that is so ambitious as to become exhausting: too many tests to give, too many tasks to monitor, and too much data to consider. A teacher who takes a "large-grain" approach—who subsumes similar, small-grain building blocks into fewer, larger ones—will need to design, administer, review, and base adjustment decisions on fewer assessments on fewer occasions. Generally speaking, a large-grain approach means a more efficient application of formative assessment.

With this in mind, when an architect is working on a learning progression, it's a good idea to look for similarities among subskills and ask if they can be combined. As when attempting to subsume lesser building blocks under a larger building block, the students' status with respect to each building block must be ascertained via some sort of assessment. So, as a potential building block is under consideration—a building block of any grain size—the learning progression's architect must constantly be asking, *"What is a practical way to assess students' status with respect to this building block?"*

Because learning progressions are most often crafted for instructional units of several weeks' duration, when deciding on the grain size of building blocks, it can be helpful for the architect to estimate how long it is likely to take for students to master the kinds of building blocks under consideration. And, given that students' mastery of each building block must be determined via some sort of assessment procedure, how much time should be allocated to such assessments? Part of the challenge in devising a crackerjack learning progression is paying attention to the time that's available and using it wisely.

Choice-Point 3: The Number of Building Blocks in the Learning Progression

This decision flows clearly from the one that precedes it. The goal for learning-progression architects is to ensure that every building block is really and truly requisite, and that each assessment administered is worthwhile.

The leaner a learning progression is, the more likely it is to be used. Heroic implementation of formative assessment using a 10-building-block learning progression is something that an ambitious and dedicated teacher might wish to take on once—prior to retirement. But, practically speaking, how likely is any teacher to continue following that progression, which means gathering assessment evidence for the purpose of instructional adjustment at 10 separate points throughout a unit of instruction? The questions for the architect to ask here are, *"What is my tolerance level for assessment and data analysis? What is my students' tolerance for assessment?"*

Choice-Point 4: What the Building Blocks Should Be

The selection of the enabling subskills and bodies of enabling knowledge for a learning progression is best informed by first thinking about how students' mastery of the target aim will be measured at the conclusion of the instruction, and then engaging in a rigorous *backwards analysis.* Here, the learning-progression architect takes the target curricular aim and asks: *"What* must *a student know or be able to do in order to master* this *aim?"* Once a clear answer to this question has emerged, a building block has been born. Then it's a matter of repeating the question, focusing on that building block: *"What must a student know or be able to do in order to master* this *building block?"* Backwards analysis permits a teacher to eventually isolate what he believes to be the truly necessary stepping stones for a student's successful journey toward mastery of the target curricular aim. Is that analysis the definitive analysis? Of course not; thoughtful people will often end up with different views of what students must know and do to learn certain things. Here, the would-be architect must be bold, think hard, apply experience-won wisdom (and colleagues' wisdom, too, if possible), and map out the best learning progression possible.

Teachers will differ in how they prefer to identify a learning progression's building blocks. After first becoming clearheaded about the nature of the target curricular aim itself, some teachers will prefer to "start from scratch" by using a backwards analysis uninfluenced by other information. On the other hand, many teachers will realize that for most curricular aims there may be useful analyses available, analyses that can be reviewed to see if they make instructional sense. Where are these analyses? Well, they can be found in the textbooks and other instructional materials supplied by publishers. If you're a teacher who's using a particular textbook in a class, you can locate the section in the book dealing with the target curricular aim you're considering and then figure out what major chunks of knowledge or what subskills the textbook's authors regard as important. You can then decide whether you should make any of these subskills or bodies of knowledge a building block in your developing learning progression.

Another potential source for building-block possibilities would be any plans a teacher already has in place for carrying out an instructional unit. Just think about the way teachers plan their instruction by laying out all the key stuff their students need to know and figuring out the order in which to present it. Well, lurking in that "key stuff" and those weekly lesson plans is an already sequenced set of must-master building blocks that can form a defensible learning progression.

By using backwards analysis and drawing on the instructional thinking of others, even novice teachers can come up with a reasonable set of building blocks. Will those building blocks always be the "right" or "best" ones? No, but fortunately learning progressions aren't set in concrete. For a teacher's next attempt to help a different group of students master a given curricular goal, a re-analyzed and revised set of building blocks can be sent into battle. Learning progressions, just like fine wine and teachers' skills, can improve over time.

Another bit of advice: When setting out to build a learning progression, it's imperative to focus on what must be taught during the instructional period under consideration—the two weeks, four weeks, two months, or other time period set aside for the instructional unit. In other words, although the backwards analysis might logically trace the pursuit of the target curriculum aim all the way back to skills and knowledge like "Students must be able to decode words" or "Students must know the multiplication tables," the building blocks in the learning progression should deal with the necessary en-route student accomplishments associated with the instruction that can realistically be provided. The myriad collection of things students have learned or should have learned in earlier units or prior grade levels are outside the scope of the learning progression.

Choice-Point 5: How the Building Blocks Will Be Sequenced

Having completed a backwards analysis, most of the sequencing work will already have been done: which skills and knowledge depend on mastery of which other skills and knowledge. This choice-point asks the learning progression's architect to take another look at the building blocks and confirm that they are in what seems to be the best order.

In the Classroom

In a fairly large Midwest school district, for more than three years, a cross-school professional learning community of social studies teachers has been working together to develop their pedagogical skills. Currently, eight high school history teachers, two social studies curriculum specialists from the district office, and one high school principal (a former history teacher) comprise the PLC. The group meets at least once per month, and sometimes twice. These meetings usually last between 90 minutes and two hours.

The PLC is currently focusing on the task of building a learning progression to help the district's social studies teachers promote students' mastery of a new and particularly challenging history goal set by the state school board:

> When presented with a fictitious current-day societal problem, students can identify from a specified series of historical events a significant occurrence with sufficient parallels to the current-day problem so that students can compose a brief essay proposing a defensible, history-based solution to the current-day problem.

In other words, this historical skill calls for students to first be able to identify an historical event that has sufficient relevance to a fictitious current-day societal problem, and then to be able to use lessons drawn from an identified occurrence associated with that historical event to generate a sound solution to the current social problem. The state's school districts were given materials to help clarify the nature of the new curricular aim, including the 20 historical events selected for study (drawn chiefly from the content of state-approved history textbooks) and up to four "significant occurrences" associated with these events. The events listed for high school U.S. history classes include, for example, the Civil War, the Industrial Revolution, America's imperialism, and the Cold War. One of the listed occurrences for the Cold War was the collapse of the Soviet Union.

During the most recent meeting of the PLC, as members were wrapping up their efforts to isolate a set of building blocks underlying this new history skill, their meeting was observed by Marla Jenson, a teacher education professor from the local state university. Marla and her colleagues are interested in stressing formative assessment with the prospective teachers in their program. But neither Marla nor many of her colleagues understand much about learning progressions or the role that progressions play in the formative assessment process. So Marla, working through a contact at the district office, got in touch with several members of the PLC and asked permission to sit in on the group's deliberations. One of the PLC members, high school history teacher Greg Cooke, agreed to talk with her after the group's most recent meeting and help clarify "what goes on when a learning progression is being born."

Key PLC Events

The PLC members met on the third Wednesday of the month, this time at West High School. After Marla Jenson introduced herself to the PLC members and explained her wish to better understand learning progressions, she sat in a chair well behind the group so she would not interfere with their work.

Jill, a 9th grade social students teacher, opened the meeting by summarizing the PLC's recent work, including how members had initially developed several assessment items to measure students' mastery of the new history skill—"our target curricular aim." Jill noted that this item-development task had taken a bit longer than PLC members had anticipated, but it had been instrumental in ensuring that all members of the team could move forward with a firm idea about what the new "Using History's Lessons Skill" actually was. One of the administrator members of the PLC agreed, saying, "As a clarification technique, I thought it was wonderful."

Jill then projected a slide showing the developing learning progression, containing two "firm" building blocks and one still up for debate:

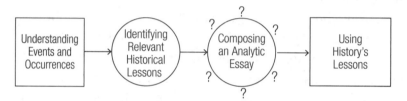

They had dubbed the first building block "Understanding Events and Occurrences," agreeing that students needed to know all of the 20 state-specified "events" and 40 or so "occurrences" within those events. Together, this would constitute a large and important knowledge-focused building block. Jill noted that students' mastery could be assessed with multiple-choice items requiring students to match events and occurrences. Follow-up assessment data on mastery might be gathered through short essays focused on describing the focal features of each event and each occurrence.

The PLC had also agreed on a second building block—a subskill focused on students' ability to select an occurrence within a historical event that is sufficiently similar to the situation embodied in a current-day societal problem. The PLC members dubbed this building block "Identifying Relevant Historical Lessons," and they had estimated that it would likely take between three and five weeks to teach. Assessment data on students' mastery might be collected via constructed-response test items to which students would need to specify *which* events' occurrence they had chosen and *why* they had selected it.

With that summary of their agreements out of the way, another PLC member, Karl, turned the group's attention to a potential building block—a subskill that Jill had introduced and defended during the PLC's most recent meeting. Karl asked Jill to recount the nature of the proposal, "for the PLC and for Professor Jenson." Jill proceeded to make her case for including explanatory essay writing as a building block. "I know we don't want the district's history teachers to turn into English teachers," Jill said, "but 'students will compose a brief essay proposing a defensible, history-based solution to the current-day problem' is right there in the standard's language. If our students don't have at least rudimentary composition skills, they will stumble when it comes to the Using History's Lessons Skill."

The PLC's members were evenly split on this proposal. At one point during a fairly heated disagreement, Jorge argued, "If we take on the obligation of teaching students to do what they should have been taught to do in their language arts classes, when are we going to have time to promote all the content the district wants us to teach—not to mention new, more powerful analytical skills like the one we've been focusing on in these meetings? Let's have English teachers teach English and history teachers teach history!"

At one point in the discussion, Jill produced a set of student papers displaying her students' abilities to write summaries of what they had read during an in-class silent read. She showed the other PLC members (and Professor Jenson) how poorly her students were writing, and again stressed her key point: "If we can't figure out *what* they've written, how will we be able to get at their cognitive mastery of the new history skill?"

After almost a full hour's discussion dealing with this proposed third building block, the meeting came to a close. One PLC member suggested that, prior to their next PLC meeting, all members "should collect opinions from other members of their schools' faculties, and not only from those who teach history, regarding the unresolved issue of the third building block."

The Interview of Greg Cooke

by Professor Marla Jenson

At the outset, Greg, I really want to express my appreciation to you and your PLC for letting me horn in on your work. As you know, most of the teacher education professors at the university are eager to build formative education into our own classes. We want to model how this process works, but we don't have any experience building learning progressions, so this was great today. I hope my presence wasn't a distraction.

On the contrary, Professor Jenson, after a few minutes, I think most of us actually forgot you were there. Believe me, what you saw today was no different from what goes on during any of our meetings. So what is it about learning progressions that you particularly want to know more about?

Oh, please call me Marla, Greg. This is really going to be an informal conversation. For openers, though, I was interested in learning how your committee had actually created assessment tasks that could be used to measure students' mastery of this new history skill. Can you go over that again for me? Do you actually intend to use the items on your tests one day?

No, Marla, we're not planning to actually use these new items, or recommend that other teachers in the district use them. The *only* purpose of writing these items was to help us get our thinking straight about what this new history standard requires students to be able to do. Although I don't think Jill mentioned it as part of her summary, during one committee meeting session we each tried to come up with our own best personal response to every sample item we had generated. Responding to and then evaluating each other's responses really helped us see far more clearly just what we were asking our students to do.

How did your PLC actually get under way in identifying what you call the learning progression's "building blocks"?

Well, as you saw, the first step was to fully clarify the nature of what it was we wanted students to be able to do at the close of instruction, which was why we created the sample items and then tried to answer them. Then, as our second step, we undertook what most folks call "a backwards analysis" that started with the target curricular aim. In this instance, that was the cognitive skill embodied in the History's Lessons standard. We simply laid out that goal, then worked backwards to identify what sorts of precursor subskills or understandings our students would need to be able to master the target skill. Backwards analysis sounds simple, but you have to be alert as you try to think what precedes what when it comes to students' learning.

Just to review a bit, tell me again about the first building block you all agreed on.

Well, although the standard is a skill—an analytical skill—it also covers a lot of historical content: 20 events and approximately 40 occurrences associated with those events. Obviously, students need to know about these events and understand the chief features of each occurrence. It's impossible to promote this sort of wide-ranging historical understanding in a week or two, or even in a month or two. So our PLC concluded that at least a full year of study could be devoted to promoting students' mastery of a knowledge-focused building block dealing with these designated events and occurrences. That's our "Understanding Events and Occurrences" building block.

Got it. And your second building block is a skill, if I recall. Did you identify it by a backwards analysis as well?

Yes, and yes we did. There was quite a bit to talk through in our group, but after a couple of meetings we concluded that our second building block would consist of a subskill, namely, the ability to isolate the key features of the fictional "current societal problem," and then choose an occurrence—from the set of 40 or so occurrences students would be learning about—that matched those salient features well enough. We refer to this second building block as "Identifying Relevant Historical Lessons." It's a really significant subskill.

Did your PLC assume that the first "knowledge" building block had to be totally mastered before teachers could start teaching this second, skill-based building block?

That's a great question. We agreed that if a student was knowledgeable about at least *some* of the events and occurrences associated with this standard, then teachers could begin to promote mastery of the second building block's subskill. For example, I might go ahead with second-building-block instruction related to early 19th-century events and occurrences before proceeding to first-building-block instruction on late 19th-century events. Accordingly, we'll probably encourage teachers to assess students' mastery of the first building block, the knowledge-focused one, at least three times during the year.

What would you say has been the most challenging part of your PLC's learning progression work?

I guess the toughest thing for us has been to resist the temptation to put lots of building blocks into our learning progression. Take the second building block—the subskill one. To master this particular building block, students have to be able to do a lot of things. They must be able to analyze the fictitious current-day problem presented to them, then they need to be able to identify a relevant *event*—such as the Industrial Revolution—and *then* they need to isolate a key *occurrence* during that event—such as the introduction of the assembly line. Well, what our subskill currently does is put all three of those smaller subskills into one coalesced larger subskill. In the early days of our deliberations, most of the PLC members wanted to present those subskills as three separate building blocks.

And why would that have been so bad?

Because we'd have been setting ourselves up for failure. That's what I think, anyway. As you may know, when carrying out formative assessment, a teacher must measure students' attainment of each and every building block. Practically speaking, that would mean creating one assessment to measure students' ability to analyze a fictitious current-day problem, another assessment to measure students' ability to identify a historical event that parallels a given problem, and a third assessment that measures their ability to isolate an occurrence within a given historical event that particularly parallels a given problem. Bear in mind that for each of these subskills to be assessed, a teacher would be designing appropriate instruction, giving the assessment, analyzing the assessment results, and adjusting instruction as needed. I know that this degree of granularity—and the amount of work it entails—might be palatable to some teachers, but if our committee came up with a learning progression containing a huge number of to-be-assessed building blocks, we'd have produced a learning progression that most district teachers would not even consider using.

I should also point out that when developing a learning progression, there's sometimes a tendency to try to coalesce everything in sight. People want to group together all the little subskills and small lumps of knowledge that seem related to the targeted curricular skill. And you also need to be careful not to coalesce fundamentally different kinds of cognitive subskills. The lesser subskills in the example we've been talking about are compatible, but if you're attempting to scrunch together skills that are not really compatible, then you're fooling yourself. For instance, in math, if Subskill A involves performing basic arithmetic operations and Subskill B requires estimating the area encompassed by various geometric problems, those two subskills don't belong together. One thing to ask yourself when you're thinking about coalescing a subskill is, "Could I assess students' mastery of the larger combined subskill with the same assessment technique?" If you'd need dramatically different kinds of assessment techniques, then you're probably trying to coalesce when you shouldn't.

Interesting. What else about building this learning progression has been challenging for your PLC?

Well, Marla, one thing we always need to keep reminding ourselves is that every building block we consider putting in our learning progression must be amenable to accurate and efficient assessment. It's so easy to get caught up in our backwards analyses that we tend to overlook the always-present assessment requirement for all building blocks.

And why is it so important not to do that?

Because this entire formative assessment enterprise is rooted in assessment-based evidence! It is easy to go rolling along and talking about all the cool things we'd like our history students to know and do, but when you start putting those cool things into building blocks—*measurable* building blocks—then you have to think hard about what's actually practical.

I guess I should add that, for me personally, the most difficult thing has been to make sure that our building blocks capture all the key subskills and knowledge a student would need to have in order to master the Using History's Lessons Skill. I want very much to come up with the *right* number of the *right* building blocks.

I see what you are saying about locating the correct building blocks, Greg. We would have trouble with that at the university, I am sure, if we were to try to carve out learning progressions for key pedagogical skills in our own teacher education program. All right, now I have to ask: How will you ever resolve the dispute that took up most of the PLC's time today? You seemed so divided on the issue of that third building block—the composition skill. There were persuasive arguments on either side of that issue, and nobody seemed willing to budge. . . .

No, they didn't, did they? OK, so take a look at the diagram of our current learning progression over there on the flip chart. As you can see, we have a target curricular aim and two very demanding building blocks. Building Block 1 consists of straightforward *knowledge*, that is, getting students to both memorize and understand some seriously large hunks of knowledge. Building Block 2 represents a sophisticated and complex cognitive subskill—composed of three lesser subskills, if you'll remember. And there's the third, under-consideration building block, surrounded by question marks.

What I have been thinking of, Marla, is asking the PLC to generate *two* learning progressions, one with a third building block and one without. Maybe we could explain the difference between the two to our colleagues and let the district's history teachers choose whichever learning progression they prefer. It just might work.

I suppose that would be a good way to go about it. Do you think your PLC would want to tackle this kind of a learning progression again? That is, can a group of educators, essentially on their own, come up with defensible learning progressions?

I think the answer is a definite *yes*. We would, and they could. Remember, the learning progression we have been struggling with represents a remarkably challenging historical skill. Not every cognitive skill is as tough as this one. Furthermore, I believe teachers are definitely up to the task of creating learning progressions for their own individual units of instruction. They won't have to worry so much about reaching consensus, for one thing, and their existing lesson plans give them a real head start when it comes to identifying the skills and knowledge that must be taught and assessed in order for students to master the unit's objectives. And, of course, every teacher can include the number of building blocks that he or she is comfortable with! And bear in mind that learning progressions, just like lesson plans, can always be improved and refined. Learning progression creation is something teacher can definitely do.

An Interview Look-Back

In this interview, we saw Professor Marla Jenson dig into many of the key issues facing those who try to create learning progressions. She started off with questions regarding the committee's efforts to clarify the target curricular aim by (1) generating actual assessment items to measure students' mastery of that aim and (2) evaluating each other's responses to those items. Such an early-on activity forces the creators of a learning progression to come to grips with precisely what it is that's being sought of students. If the architects of a learning progression do not have a clear and common under-standing of a target curricular aim, the likelihood of their ending up with a defensible learning progression is minimal.

In response to the professor's inquiry, Greg indicated that the PLC had trouble getting some members to resist tossing too many building blocks into the progression. Greg also pointed out the importance, and the occasional difficulty, of the committee's mak-ing sure that the potential for practicable assessment methods was always present. The whole mission of a learning progression is to help identify the moments when assessment evidence should be gathered. During the creation of sound learning progressions, it is rare that there can be too much attention given to the realistic assessment possibilities associated with each of its building blocks.

You will find in forthcoming chapters that almost any worthwhile application of formative assessment is dependent on the availability of a serviceable learning progression. Learning progressions, developed by educators on the basis of their best backwards analyses of what's needed by students, will not always be perfect. But without such learning progressions as blueprints for planning when and how to collect evidence of students' current status, formative assessment is almost certain to misfire.

Reflection Questions

1. What are the advantages and disadvantages of teachers' devising learning progressions by themselves versus designing them with others?

2. If you were offering guidance to a group of teachers trying to select curricular aims suitable for formative assessment, what advice would you give?

3. What do you see as the pros and cons of the "large-grain" approach to learning progression development—coalescing separate, smaller-scope subskills into larger, broader-scope subskills? Try to come up with some examples of "small-grain" subskills that should and should not be combined.

4. How would you go about persuading a group of teachers that learning progressions are indispensable to a properly conceived implementation of formative assessment?

5. Which of your current curricular aims seem like good candidates for formative assessment, and why? Take a look at your plans for a unit (or units), and see if you can map out a learning progression for it.

3

Immediate Instructional Adjustments Based on Assessed Performance

In the *immediate instructional adjustment* application of formative assessment, teachers gather assessment evidence, analyze that evidence, and change their teaching tactics (if a change is warranted) *right then*, within the same class session. Because immediate instructional adjustments by teachers can be based either on assessments of students' performance or on students' self-reported levels of understanding, we'll be considering each of these sorts of adjustments separately, in different chapters. The focus here, in Chapter 3, will be immediate adjustments based on data gathered via fairly conventional kinds of classroom assessments.

Implementation Considerations

It is difficult to argue with the instructional virtues of immediacy; any sort of self-correcting system is certain to work better if along-the-way corrections are made as quickly as possible. If we were to fantasize about the way this particular application of formative assessment might work in a pedagogical paradise, teachers would use a medley of brief assessments to gauge students' status on a continual basis—perhaps several times during each class session—and then make instant, adroit instructional adjustments as required so students would be on the receiving end of constantly perfected, truly tailored instruction.

If the data indicate that students are getting what the teacher thinks they should be getting at this stage in the instruction, then the natural conclusion is that instruction is working pretty well. No change is required, and the class session can continue as planned. But if the evidence indicates (1) students are misunderstanding the instruction; (2) students haven't "gotten it at all" yet—that is, their pace of mastery is slower than anticipated; or (3) students have already reached the level of understanding the lesson is aiming for and have none of the questions or confusion the teacher has anticipated and planned to address, then an adjustment is necessary. It is definitely time for the teacher to invoke the hoped-for virtues of Instructional Plan B, Plan C, or whatever other approach the teacher may have ready to go. These alternate plans typically entail either *more instruction* or *different instruction*—and sometimes both. In instances when students' assessment evidence indicates they have already mastered whatever's being taught, the adjustment might even be to provide *less* instruction than the teacher had planned—to skip ahead to the next topic, say, rather than distribute an apparently unneeded set of skill-building experiences. Of course, as this formative assessment application's name implies, any adjustments to be made will be immediate.

But flipping from fantasy to reality, a real-world teacher must *prepare* for any kind of en-route evidence gathering and also *be ready* to make immediate instructional adjustments depending on the nature of the evidence collected. That kind of preparation takes time, and plenty of it. It means having to identifying *when* to assess students—that is, at which point in an instructional sequence and how often in an instructional sequence. It also means figuring out *how* to assess students so that the data generated will support immediate and accurate diagnosis of students' learning status and then deciding *what* will happen instructionally, depending on the nature of the assessment results. As you can see, good teachers must be very deliberate about choosing to use this particular application of formative assessment lest they become overwhelmed and disenchanted.

This Application's Key Choice-Points

There are five key choices facing teachers who are trying to decide whether to employ formative assessment for immediate instructional adjustments based on assessed performance data. Figure 3.1 provides an overview and a preview of the nature of each decision at stake.

FIGURE 3.1

Five Choice-Points for Using Formative Assessment to Make an Immediate Instructional Adjustment Based on Performance Data

1. **What kind of assessment tool to use.** What technique or techniques will be used to ascertain students' current status?

2. **When to collect assessment evidence.** How often—and at which points during the instructional plan—will assessment evidence be collected?

3. **How many items to include in the assessment.** What number of test items will be sufficient to accurately measure student mastery of each subskill or body of knowledge being assessed?

4. **When to make an instructional adjustment.** What performance level will signal the need for an instructional adjustment?

5. **What kind of instructional adjustment to make.** If students' performance level indicates instructional adjustment is necessary, what adjustment will be at the ready?

Choice-Point 1: What Kind of Assessment Tool to Use

The thrust of the immediate-adjustment application of formative assessment requires the teacher to be able to gain a very quick measurement of students' status. This means setting aside pencil-and-paper quizzes and the like in favor of evidence-gathering that can be done with just a few questions and a visual survey of student responses.

There are some fancy electronic response systems on the market capable of tallying and providing instant summaries of students' multiple-choice answers, but I want to focus on the more common (and budget friendly) techniques: (1) the *thumbs-up/down procedure*, (2) *letter-card responses*, and (3) *whiteboard responses.*

The thumbs-up/down procedure. This simple signaling technique involves the teacher's presenting the class with binary-choice questions—True/False or Right/Wrong test items. The teacher presents a question orally, on the chalkboard, or via a projection device. Then the students, at the teacher's prompt, display their answer by holding a thumb up (for "True") or a thumb down (for "False") in front of their chests, where the teacher can see the signal but classmates cannot. The teacher then scans the direction of students' extended thumbs and takes a rough tally of how many students have answered correctly. Based on the ratio of correct responses to incorrect responses, the teacher decides whether an instructional adjustment is in order.

A clear advantage of the thumbs-up/down procedure approach is that it doesn't require any additional materials, as the vast majority of students come equipped with at least one thumb. Because the teacher uses two-choice questions, it's usually possible to present these questions orally rather than write them on the chalkboard or present them on a display screen. However, the yes-or-no question format does have its drawbacks. Binary-choice test items, if not created with care, can easily slip into measuring nothing more than memorized information and, thus, encourage student thinking at lower rather than higher levels of cognition. Elsewhere (Popham, 2011), I have described how to create binary-choice items that elicit more than merely memorized information.

Letter-card responses. This is a straightforward technique built on students' instant responses to prepared multiple-choice questions. As its name implies, a letter-card system requires the teacher to provide students with pieces of cardstock (often standard index cards, white and approximately 5 by 8 inches in size), on which are printed large letters of the response options the teacher wants students to be able to make. The most common use of letter-cards involves letters A to E, and some teachers include a question mark card students can use to indicate uncertainty.

As with the thumbs-up/down procedure, the teacher signals students when to raise their cards (so the teacher can see but other students can't), visually discerns what the students' response patterns are, and tells the students when "Cards down" is in order.

This technique's use of multiple-choice questions is one of its chief virtues. A teacher may design multiple-choice items to tease out very finely shaded pictures of understanding via answer-options that convey subtle differences in "correctness." In addition, some wrong-answer options can be structured so that when students choose certain of these "distracters," as they're often called, those responses signify a particular kind of confusion that can be addressed instructionally.

Yes, there's a bit more preparation involved with this assessment technique. Obviously, teachers must procure and create the cards, but they must also post or display each question along with all its possible answer options so that students don't have to rely on their memories to keep straight which letter is associated with which answer. Students who can't remember which letter corresponds to their intended answer won't generate accurate assessment data. Another consideration, which applies to any kind of selected-response test item, is that reliance on a letter-card technique does restrict a teacher to presenting questions for which students select an answer from presented options rather than being obliged to generate their answers "from scratch." Certain sorts of subskills really require students not merely to select a response from alternatives but, instead, to come up with an original response. We see this when students must be able to coalesce apparently disparate dollops of information into some kind of brand new cognitive casserole. To find out how well students can do such coalescing on their own, letter-cards are simply inadequate.

Whiteboard responses. This third quick-assessment technique is the answer when a teacher seeks a constructed response. Students respond to teacher questions by writing a word or a brief phrase on individual, tablet-sized, erasable whiteboards, and then present their answers in the usual way when the teacher calls for "Whiteboards up!" (Rags or old socks, preferably clean ones, can be used to erase old responses and prepare the board for its next use.) The challenge of using whiteboards is that the teacher must limit questions to those that can be answered satisfactorily through a single word or short phrase. Remember, the teacher is looking to gather data on student understanding via a quick visual scan.

To sum up, then, the questions a teacher needs to ask when facing this choice-point are *"How much preparation time do I have?"* and *"What kind of data am I looking for—a general sense of whether students 'get it' or not, or am I looking for more diagnostic information?"* And, of course, although there's no reason for teachers to limit themselves to a single data-gathering approach, most teachers who adopt this particular application of formative assessment tend to employ one of the approaches more than others; they become familiar with a particular response system, and so do their students.

In choosing among these three alternatives for collecting assessment evidence, the overriding concern is always the same—namely, what sorts of assessment approach will generate the data that will support the most *valid* inferences about students' status? If a less elaborate approach will do the assessment job well, then there's little need for a more elaborate approach.

Choice-Point 2: When to Collect Assessment Evidence

As stated, I believe teachers must collect assessment evidence for each building block in the learning progression they are using— optimally, near the conclusion of instruction focused on the building block, but while there is still some time available for any assessment-dictated adjustments to right instructional wrongs. However, each teacher's affinity for assessment will be different. Some teachers may want to collect data on students' achievement of less significant sorts of en-route accomplishments that will contribute to building

block mastery—what we might call the "subgoals" or "subcomponents" of the subskills or bodies of enabling knowledge.

A teacher's decision about how *often* to collect assessment evidence to inform an instant adjustment will almost always interact
with the teacher's choice of *how* to collect that evidence. Certain
data-gathering techniques are higher on the "hassle index" than others. For instance, a thumbs-up/down procedure is likely to require
less preparation and administration time than a whiteboard procedure will. The "how often" decision is also affect by factors such
as the students' level of background knowledge, the complexity
of the subject matter at hand (more complicated subject matter
means more opportunities for student-stumbles), and how much
experience the teacher has with the subject matter (the better a
teacher knows the material and the ways in which students are
likely to misunderstand it, the less onerous the prep work required
for immediate-adjustment formative assessment will be). During a
five-week teaching unit, for example, some teachers may be quite
satisfied to employ immediate-adjustment formative assessment
only three or four times. Other teachers embarking on the same
five-week unit might wish to assess students two or three times each
week, focusing not only on students' mastery of a learning progression's building blocks, but also on students' grasp of numerous, less
significant knowledge and skills. Here, the teacher needs to ask,
*"When, during the instructional sequence I have planned, would
it make the most sense to make an instructional adjustment?"* and
*"What effect would pausing to collect assessment evidence have on
the planned instructional sequence?"*

The third question to ask at this choice-point is one that, frankly,
should trump the instructional and assessment considerations
raised by the first two questions. That question is, *"How willing am
I to do this?"* The best advice I can give to teachers here is that they
must be honest about both their assessment time and inclination,
and they must beware of setting an evidence-gathering schedule
that is so demanding that it will lead them to abandon the entire
formative assessment enterprise. Several teachers have told me

about how they initially tried to use immediate-adjustment formative assessment every day in their classes. After all, it doesn't seem like such a big deal to call for thumbs-up/thumbs-down measures of understanding. But, because these folks were dedicated to doing formative assessment right, they also diligently prepared sets of instructional adjustments to have at the ready, depending on what the assessment data revealed—thus doubling or tripling their preparation burden. It wasn't too long before these teachers found themselves cutting back their formative assessment frequency on the grounds of sanity preservation.

If I were teaching high school students again and considering when to collect assessment evidence for the purpose of making immediate instructional adjustments process, although I'd be influenced by instructional and assessment considerations, I'd make my decision chiefly on the basis of the third factor—namely, my own tolerance for such evidence gathering.

Choice-Point 3: How Many Items to Include in the Assessment

A teacher's task here is to figure out how many assessment items are enough to generate good data on students' mastery status relative to the subskill or body of enabling knowledge being assessed. The two key factors to consider are the building block's breadth (its grain size) and the relative importance of that building block to a student's overall mastery of the target curricular aim. Although all building blocks in a learning progression are crucial, some are "more crucial" than others. The larger the grain size of the building block in question, and the more crucial it is to mastery, the more items the teacher will need to make a sound adjust-or-don't-adjust decision.

The rationale for using more items for larger building blocks is a simple one: with more content subsumed in a building block, there is more content mastery to measure, and more items that must be written. By contrast, a teacher might measure mastery of a small-grained building block covering an important but simple concept with a single, well-crafted question.

The exact number of items to include in an assessment is a teacher's judgment call. If the teacher thinks that one or two items are too few, but that three or four items will provide a sufficiently accurate estimate of students' status, then the teacher should opt for the larger number of items. Here, the question to ask is, *"How much data would I need to be comfortable deciding that a student either has or has not mastered this building block?"*

Choice-Point 4: When to Make an Instructional Adjustment

In *TA1*, I recommended that before collecting evidence of students' status, teachers should carefully think through what level of performance would signal, "Instructional adjustment is necessary." (Setting adjustment triggers *after* data collection tends to increase the frequency of concluding that students' performance is "good enough.")

The trick to formulating an adjustment trigger is to first set a required level for individual student performance and then spell out a required level for the whole class. To illustrate, a teacher might decide that the baseline of individual mastery for a certain subskill will be providing a correct thumbs-up/thumbs-down response to five of six questions, and that the adjustment trigger will be three-fourths of the class failing to reach this mastery level. In other words, the teacher might make a note that "if at least three-fourths of the class do not answer five or six of the items correctly, I will make an instructional adjustment."

The guiding principle in determining adjustment-trigger levels flows from the relative instructional importance of whatever subskill or body of knowledge the assessment is measuring. Really important subskills and enabling knowledge need more stringent performance levels than less important ones do—both in terms of the performance level established for an individual student and with regard to the "percent successful" performance level set for the entire group of students.

Choice-Point 5: What Kind of Instructional Adjustment to Make

Ultimately, it all comes down to this. Remember, the essence of this application of formative assessment is the teacher's making an immediate instructional adjustment. The instantaneity of the adjustment means that the teacher must have planned what to do and be ready to implement that adjusted instruction *immediately.*

Margaret Heritage, a colleague of mine at UCLA, works frequently with teachers who are trying to employ formative assessment. She finds that the most difficult choice they face is figuring out what to do *after* assessment evidence has shown them that an instructional adjustment is needed (Heritage, Kim, Vendlinski, & Herman, 2009). It seems, therefore, that teachers might wish to prepare a template filled in with a variety of fix-it possibilities that make instructional sense to them. This template might be similar to Figure 3.2, which identifies potential sources of students' confusion a teacher ought to consider when deciding how to make adjustments if assessment evidence reveals less-than-effective instruction.

The adjustment possibilities in this figure are illustrative, not definitive. In truth, the diversity of curricular aims, the composition of student groups, teachers' personal pedagogical styles, and a carload of contextual differences make it altogether impossible to prescribe what teachers should do when adjusting unsuccessful instruction. It is always possible that factors other than those captured in the figure will contribute to a given group of students' misconceptions and to less-than-satisfactory mastery of whatever the teacher has assessed. But let me stress again that a teacher employing this particular brand of formative assessment needs to have all possible Plans B, C, and so on prepared and ready to roll out if needed. A set of ideas such as those in the figure, informed by the teacher's own past pedagogical experiences, can provide useful starting points for these planning efforts.

FIGURE 3.2

Potential Adjustment Possibilities

Possible Source of Confusion	Sample Options for Instructional Adjustments
My explanation of the key content was not clear.	*Re-explain, using* . . . different metaphors or examples. . . . a different mode of instruction (e.g., visual/aural).
Students don't understand what they're supposed to be working toward.	*Clarify the intended outcome of instruction by* . . . talking about the nature of the target curricular aim. . . . focusing on evaluative criteria that will be used to judge the quality of their performance.
My learning progression has shortcomings.	*Review prior learning progression choices by* . . . determining if any earlier key building blocks have been omitted. . . . deciding if adjustment-trigger levels for previous building blocks were too low.
Students have not received adequate modeling.	*Provide additional modeling by* . . . distributing and using a detailed rubric or performance model. . . . conducting a demonstration. . . . assigning heterogeneous pairwork in which a struggling student works with a buddy who has mastered the content.
Students have not had sufficient time on task.	*Provide additional guided or independent practice by* . . . setting small-group practice activities. . . . assigning new homework problems.

Having introduced you to the key ingredients in this application of the formative assessment process, let's look now at a teacher who is using it in her classroom.

In the Classroom

Alice Olson teaches world and U.S. history at Edison High School, a large urban secondary school in New England that draws students from a wide range of socioeconomic strata and ethnicities. This is Alice's sixth year of teaching and her fourth year at Edison. Although several of her colleagues use formative assessment in their classes, Alice is regarded by the rest of the faculty as the school's most knowledgeable user of formative assessment.

This year, Edison High School has a brand new principal, Kevin Todd. By his own admission, Kevin possesses almost no experience working with teachers who employ the formative assessment process, and he's eager to educate himself on its use. Alice has agreed to have one of her classes videotaped so that her principal can see formative assessment in action. This is no big deal, she assures him; at Edison, classes are routinely videotaped by students in the school's advanced technology program so that various lessons and instructional approaches can be reviewed by faculty members working in professional learning communities. Because of the considerable frequency with which these video recordings are made, most students have become quite inured to them and rarely "play to the camera."

So the following Tuesday morning, during a lesson about the Civil War, a video recording is made of Alice's second period 11th grade U.S. history class. Copies of the video are delivered to Principal Todd and Alice by Wednesday afternoon. They both watch the video prior to their after-school interview on Friday, during which they review several segments together.

Key Classroom Events

The video recording opens with a lively, teacher-led discussion of the potential causes of the Civil War. The questions Alice poses for her students are not fact-focused questions but a series of why-type queries, and most of the students take an active part in trying to resolve the sometimes subtle issues they present. After about 15 minutes of this open-class discussion, Alice asks her students to take out their A-B-C-D letter-cards because, as she announces, she wants to collect formative assessment evidence about certain aspects of the Civil War "as seen through your eyes."

At that point in the class session, students take a set of 6-by-9-inch cards from their desks. Alice then uses a computer-controlled projector to show five multiple-choice questions, one at a time. After students have had a chance to consider a question for a few moments, Alice says, "Cards up!" and students hold up one of their letter-cards so that it's visible to her but not to their classmates. Alice scans the room, quickly jots down a tabulation of students' responses, then says, "Cards down." This process continues for all five questions, at which point Alice looks at her notes regarding students' responses, thanks the students for their cooperation, then announces, "Based on the answers you've provided, we're going to do a little shifting in what I had previously planned."

"All right," Alice continues, "I'm passing out a copy of an editorial that appeared two years ago in the *Boston Globe*, but its message is every bit as pertinent today as it was then. Please read the editorial carefully, then write a summary of 25 words or less that captures the editorial's central message. We'll take 15 minutes for this, and then I'll choose three of you—using our regular random-selection procedure—to read your summaries aloud. Everyone understand? OK, then. Please begin now."

When the allotted time has passed, Alice asks for everyone's attention and then calls on three students, one after the other. The summaries they read are very similar. The essence of the editorial is that Northerners often adopt a simplistic, uninformed explanation about the cause of the Civil War, ascribing it exclusively to "the South's wanting to retain its slaves." The editorial contends that the underlying causes of the Civil War were far more complicated than merely the slavery issue, and that today's Northerners have an obligation to understand the full range of events and motives that fostered this remarkably bloody conflict.

The class session closes with students working in study groups of three or four to identify at least a half-dozen factors that led to the Civil War. Meanwhile, Alice posts written instructions for the evening's homework assignment, which she reads aloud just prior to the bell: "Tonight, please read the previously assigned textbook pages covering the root causes of the Civil War and be prepared to look more closely at what led to a conflict in which so many Southerners and Northerners lost their lives."

The Interview of Alice Olson

by Principal Kevin Todd

Alice, thanks so much for agreeing to have your class recorded and for allowing me to look at the video. To get under way, I thought you did a wonderful job with your students, and they obviously were fully engaged in what was going on. But we're here to focus on formative assessment, so let's do that. Now, I assume that formative assessment was what took place when you asked your students to respond to those five multiple-choice questions, the ones you projected on the screen. Is that right?

Well, Kevin, yes, you're almost right! The five questions were *part* of the formative assessment process. It is that last word, *process*, that's really key. The evidence I collected from students—the evidence they supplied with their letter-card answers to the five questions—was an important part of the process. But the process continues beyond that to include my deciding, based on this evidence, whether to make an instructional adjustment and what instructional adjustment to make.

OK, yes, I saw that you initiated the activity based on the Boston Globe *editorial right after you saw how the kids responded to your multiple-choice items. Did you decide to assign that activity based on those answers?*

Yes, I did. My original plan had been to spend the second half of that class session on foreign involvement in the Civil War, and if a prespecified proportion of my students had answered all of the relevant items correctly, that's exactly what I would have done. Actually, only three of the five multiple-choice questions were related to my decision to launch the editorial activity. Those were Questions 1, 2, and 3, which I wrote specifically to generate evidence about the kids' understanding of the causes of the Civil War. Questions 4 and 5 dealt with another aspect of my instruction, the initial military strength of the Northern and Southern forces. Fortunately, almost all of the students did really well on those other two questions, but if they hadn't, the adjustment I had in my pocket was to re-explain the key military-strength differences in a different way. I had the outline for that re-explanation in my notes.

As for the instructional adjustment I did make? Well, I'm from Arizona originally, and when I first moved here, to New England, I read two articles by history professors talking about a "Northern take" on the causes of the Civil War. They argued that teachers in New England needed to go the extra mile to make sure their students acquired a balanced and accurate view of this aspect of U.S. history.

Tell me more about how you could tell from the class response to those three questions that your students had this "Northern take" on the war's causes.

There's a lot you can do with multiple-choice questions! I wrote each of these questions to include one correct answer choice—a response capturing the understanding I want my students to acquire—and three wrong answers. But for each question, I designed one of the wrong-answer options to reflect the "Northern take." Here, see, for Question 1, it was Option A; for Question 2, it was Option B; and for Question 3, it was Option C. All I did, when I scanned the room for the students' answers, was mentally calculate the approximate proportion of my students who were incorrect, and then what proportion of those erring students had chosen the Northern-take responses for those three items.

How many wrong responses and "Northern take" responses were "too many"? In other words, how did you decide what levels of misunderstanding would mean making an instructional change?

That's a good question, and I can tell you it's sometimes really tough to decide how bad is "bad enough" to require an instructional adjustment. It's something that I spend time considering during my planning, and I jot down notes next to each question about where the tipping points are. When I first began using formative assessment, I tended to be too optimistic about whether my instruction would work the way I had planned for it to work, and I was constantly setting levels for my students that were pretty high—you know, "Ninety percent of the students will answer 90 percent of questions correctly." I found that I was in a constant state of adjustment, which was exhausting. I've gotten better at setting performance levels now. It comes with experience, I think.

What were the change-determining levels you set for those three questions we were talking about? And how about for last two questions, the ones that students did well enough on not to trigger an adjustment?

That's what we call them, you know, "adjustment triggers." Well, starting with your second question, you can see in my notes here that I'd decided that if at least 80 percent of my class did not answer both Question 4 and Question 5 correctly, I would make the planned adjustment, which was to provide a different kind of explanation than the one I'd given earlier. As it turned out, almost 100 percent of the class came up with the correct letter-card responses to those two questions, so there was no need for an adjustment.

On Questions 1, 2, and 3, I had decided that if two-thirds of the class did not answer all three questions correctly, then I'd look further at their wrong-answer responses, to see if more than half of those who missed those questions had opted for the incorrect "Northern-take" response. If that happened, and it definitely did, I was ready to introduce the *Boston Globe* editorial activity.

So if less than half of the class had gone for those Northern-take responses you wouldn't have made that adjustment?

I'd have made *an* adjustment, but not that particular adjustment, which was a response designed to address a particular misunderstanding, a particular barrier to mastery. If my students had flopped on the three key questions but had *not* chosen the Northern-take options in the numbers that they did, I would have gone back to re-explain the generally accepted causes underlying the Civil War.

Actually, what we're talking about now is a very significant part of making on-the-spot instructional adjustments. The teacher has to scan student responses really quickly—within seconds, really. For the three questions we've been talking about, I had to first determine the students' percent of mistakes, and then figure out how many students had opted for the Northern-take distracters. When I'm scanning the collection of letter-cards in a large class, it's about making the most accurate estimate possible and then using that data to choose the most appropriate adjustment from a set of adjustments I'm prepared to make.

Do you remember those "choose your own adventure" books? They were big when I was in elementary school. These are books in which the author presents a scenario and then asks the reader make a choice: "You walk down the hallway of the haunted house and see two doors: Do you want to open the red door or the black door? If you choose the red door, turn to page 15; if you choose the black door, turn to page 17." Well, applying formative assessment to make immediate instructional adjustments is like writing one of those books. You have to map out the various ways students might respond, and then be prepared with the right instructional adjustment depending on how they *do* respond.

OK, what you just explained brings up a good question. How often do you apply formative assessment in this way? There seems to be a lot of planning and preparation involved. Surely, Alice, you can't be doing this sort of thing every day—or can you?

Believe it or not, some teachers do. It's an issue that I've personally had trouble resolving. When I first began to use the formative assessment process—that was about four years ago—I knew I wanted to take frequent readings of students' progress. I would look at my lesson plans and, based on those plans, map out some reasonable learning progressions. Then I'd see where I might collect evidence related to the mastery of each subskill and each knowledge-focused building block in those progressions. I wound up deciding I'd need to gather assessment data every two or three weeks at minimum—slightly before the conclusion of instruction based on each building block. Well, I was so gung ho about formative assessment that I wanted to do frequent monitoring. The idea was to catch kids as they were just beginning to get off course and get them back *on* course. So I started using the letter-card assessments for immediate instructional adjustment once a week, assessing not just the building blocks but also the subcomponents of those building blocks—the things that students needed to know and be able to do to master the building blocks! What I found, though, was that it was positively overwhelming—and so time-consuming.

So what did you do then?

I cut back. Here's the thing: I believe in the power of formative assessment, and I didn't want to burn out on it. After all, *I* was the one who'd set it up to be so difficult for myself. Today, I think

I have a system that works for me. I still prepare assessments for each of the building blocks in any unit that will last three weeks or more. Beyond the building block tests, however, I'm a bit more restrained when it comes to collecting assessment evidence of the lesser subgoals.

But you still assess some subgoals? How do you decide which subgoals to assess?

Yes, I do, and I decide based on experience, mostly. I focus on aspects of the content that have tripped up students in the past. Actually, that's what you saw in Tuesday's lesson. I wasn't assessing students' mastery of a learning progression's building block; I was measuring a lesser understanding that I suspected would get in the way of building block mastery.

If I were to encourage more of Edison's teachers to try out formative assessment in their own classes, Alice, would you be willing to help them arrive at a reasonable way to decide when to collect assessment evidence from their students?

Absolutely! But I'd want to make it clear that the frequency of data gathering depends, in very important ways, on an individual teacher's preferences. Sure, we need to know whether kids have mastered all the along-the-way building blocks, and in this application of formative assessment—the immediate-adjustment type—we need to be ready to launch into a different instructional activity if they haven't. But beyond that required amount of assessment, formative assessment really hinges on what a teacher is *personally* comfortable doing. Some people may be really happy and comfortable incorporating this kind of formative assessment into every class session, but it's not the best choice for me.

One other thing I should point out, Kevin: I never grade my students on any of these letter-card assessments, and I try to help them understand that the purpose of these assessments is to help

me figure out how to teach them as well as I can. It's about them
supplying me with the assessment evidence I need to do a better
job—*for them*. I think getting this take on classroom assessment
across to students is a particularly positive consequence of the
formative assessment process. They are, in a real sense, partnering
with me to sharpen my ongoing instruction.

An Interview Look-Back

Interviews are akin to ink blots, and different people see different
things when reviewing what goes on in most interviews. You are
apt to have focused on something different than I did, but I believe
Alice's comments should have alerted her principal to three important considerations for a teacher trying to apply formative assessment for the purpose of immediate instructional adjustments.

First, there was the issue of how well students had to perform on
an in-class assessment so a teacher would know that an instructional
adjustment was warranted. As Alice said, this is a tough choice
and, even if a decision is made in advance, the decision may still
be made in error. It's a teacher's judgment call, and Alice said her
earlier estimates regarding students' likely performance had been
too high. Fortunately, experience is a marvelous helper here. Seasoned teachers tend to have solid expectations regarding students'
necessary levels of understanding, and they can be a good source
of information for less-seasoned teachers.

Second, Kevin, the principal, sensibly dug into the "How often?"
question—a tricky one. Alice stressed that a range in the frequency
of assessments is possible—from a minimum focusing solely on a
learning progression's building blocks all the way to almost-daily
assessments. Alice has apparently chosen a middle stance, in which
she makes sure to assess students' building block mastery but also
tries to check on mastery of certain less-important curricular aims.

Finally, what came up several times in the interview was Alice's
candid concern about the danger of making formative assessment
so difficult that it becomes aversive. All sorts of refinements in

formative assessment will not benefit students if teachers find the formative assessment process so onerous that they never use it.

Remember, *there is no single best way to make formative assessment fly.* Other teachers might well have made other decisions than Alice did. But as long as teachers adhere to the core concepts of formative assessment, those teachers' students will usually be successful.

Reflection Questions

1. The first application of formative assessment involves a teacher's making immediate instructional adjustments on the basis of evidence garnered by assessing students through the use of (1) a thumbs-up/down procedure, (2) letter-card responses, or (3) whiteboard responses. These assessment techniques permit teachers to make essentially instantaneous decisions regarding whether to adjust instruction. How important do you think immediacy is when making an adjustment decision? Why?

2. If you were recommending one of the three assessment procedures treated in the chapter to a teacher who was just beginning to use formative assessment, which one would you suggest. Why?

3. What are the strengths and weaknesses of this application of formative assessment? If you were charged with convincing your colleagues to give this kind of formative assessment a try, what argument would you make?

4. Take a look at the illustrative adjustment options in Figure 3.2 and think of a unit that you teach. What other points of confusion might there be in that unit, and what are some of the instructional adjustments you might make? Consider both the students you teach and your own pedagogical preferences.

4

Immediate Instructional Adjustments Based on Student-Reported Understanding

We turn now to a slightly different version of immediate-adjustment formative assessment. Here, the teacher installs a system whereby students can signal how well they believe they understand what's taking place in class. If students' self-reported levels of understanding are sufficiently high, the teacher merrily proceeds with previously planned instructional activities. However, if students' self-reported levels of understanding are low—that is, if a certain number of students report *not* comprehending what's going on—then the teacher makes an immediate instructional adjustment. It's just that simple.

Implementation Considerations

The immediate-adjustment application of formative assessment requires teachers to arrive at positive answers to the following two questions: (1) Do students really know what they understand and don't understand? (2) If they do, will they honestly report that understanding or lack of understanding? For instance, will Molly Miller—who rarely shines academically—be willing to reveal when she is absolutely lost during the teacher's current explanation? Will Jason Jones, widely regarded as the smartest kid in his classes, be willing to parade his almost-constant understanding of what's transpiring in class, marking himself as a "show-off"? In short, even if students *can* be trained to be pretty much on-target about what they know and don't know, will they be forthright in reporting it?

This Application's Key Choice-Points

As with immediate-adjustment decisions based on conventional assessments of students' performances, this variation of formative assessment also presents teachers with a collection of key decisions. Several are identical to those we discussed in reference to conventional assessment, but two are significantly different. You can get a preview of the six choice-points in Figure 4.1.

FIGURE 4.1
_____

Six Choice-Points for Using Formative Assessment to Make an Immediate Instructional Adjustment Based on Students' Self-Reported Understanding

1. **What kind of assessment tool to use.** Which self-report procedure(s) will students use to signal their levels of understanding?

2. **When to collect assessment evidence.** How often—and during which segments of instruction—will students be asked to signal their understanding?

3. **How to help students more accurately self-assess their understanding.** What strategies will be used to improve students' ability to self-assess? What will be done to foster students' metacognitive insight?

4. **When to make an instructional adjustment.** What degree of reported misunderstanding will signal the need for an instructional adjustment?

5. **What kind of instructional adjustment to make.** If students' self-reports indicate instructional adjustment is necessary, what adjustment options will be at the ready?

6. **How to help students more honestly report their understanding.** What strategies will be used to increase students' willingness to be candid about their true level of understanding?

Choice-Point 1: What Kind of Assessment Tool to Use

As this application of formative assessment is based on students' signaling teachers about their current levels of understanding, the first decision teachers must make is how students will do that. The ideal approach is a three-level signal system, in which the students can communicate (1) "I understand what's going on," (2) "I'm somewhat uncertain about what's going on," or (3) "I definitely do not understand what's going on." In a perfect world—one in which every student's desk is equipped with an electronic signaling device—the teacher would be able to see these signals but other students would not. In *our* world, most teachers who use this application of formative assessment rely on students to display green, red, or yellow cards, pieces of paper, or plastic drinking cups.

In *TA1*, I provided some detail on this "traffic-signal" technique, so named because students use these color-coded props to communicate traffic-signal-equivalent messages about their level of understanding. Green indicates, "Go on! I understand"; yellow indicates, "Caution! I'm uncertain about this"; and red indicates, "Stop! I do not understand."

Although almost any kind of material can be used for this purpose, cards or cups are particularly popular among teachers who use this application of formative assessment. Several teachers have mentioned to me that color-cards laid flat on a desktop or workstation are less visible to other students than cups are. For this reason, a number of teachers prefer cards to cups, believing students are more willing to signal their lack of understanding when they don't have worry as much about the judgment of their peers.

Typically, evidence collection begins with all students placing their cards/cups so that the green one is on top, the yellow one is next, and the red one is at the bottom. Then students are directed to change their top card/cup from green to yellow or red whenever their levels of understanding diminish. Although teachers ordinarily need to spend some time explaining and modeling how to use the green/yellow/red signals, most students catch on fairly quickly to what's involved in this self-report process.

Choice-Point 2: When to Collect Assessment Evidence

A second choice-point for a teacher using this kind of formative assessment involves a decision about *when* to employ signaling systems. Generally speaking, this approach is well suited for instances when the teacher is giving an explanation—say, during a whole-class discussion or a lecture. Self-report signaling might also be used while students are working independently on application exercises, or when they are working collaboratively in small groups and need to summon the teacher for clarification or redirection. Such clarifications and redirections constitute immediate instructional adjustments on the teacher's part. Unlike the teacher prompts and questions that always kick off evidence gathering via assessed performance, self-reporting is often student-directed and ongoing throughout a lesson; students report their status as they become aware of that status.

At one extreme, we find teachers who make this kind of signaling system *always* available to their students, from the opening seconds of a class period right up until the end-of-class bell. At the other extreme, a teacher might restrict use of a signaling system to key occasions, such as class sessions focused on explaining important new concepts, when it's essential to monitor how those explanations are being received by students. Once again, there is *no one best way* for a teacher to use formative assessment. The question a teacher must ask is, *"What approach seems most likely to work in my particular situation, given the students involved, the subject matter, the school leadership, and my own teaching style?"*

Choice-Point 3: How to Help Students More Accurately Self-Assess Their Understanding

Although most adults are pretty good at discerning how well they understand something, children haven't had the time to get to know themselves quite so well. Accordingly, teachers who use this application of formative assessment need to give some serious thought to how to sharpen the accuracy of students' self-assessment.

Teaching metacognition—the awareness and understanding of one's own thought processes—is a sound and popular approach to this challenge. A teacher might, for instance, focus students on what it means to understand something. How do they *know* when they "get" something? By being about to talk or write about it comfortably? By being able to answer questions about it without feeling nervous or anxious? Together, the teacher and students might create a rubric that identifies the qualities of a true, honest-to-goodness understanding of anything, which the students would go on to use to guide judgments about *their own* levels of understanding. For more suggestions on how to teach metacognition, see Pellegrino and Goldman (2007), Heritage (2010), and Cooper and Jenson (2009).

Another possibility worth exploring is for teachers to provide "talk-through" explanations of how they personally gauge their understanding of new information or experiences. Clearly, teachers will vary in the ways they search for certitude in such instances, and teachers always need to stress the potential variety of options open to students. However, when a teacher talks through the process of moving from less uncertainty to more uncertainty, it is often not only illustrative to students but quite comforting as well. It's valuable for students to grasp that even adults aren't instantly able to determine if they know something—and adults can be wrong.

In a sense, teachers might consider treating the topic of self-assessment as a bona fide curricular goal. Doing so might involve a teacher clarifying that intention so students know what's being sought of them, supplying some expository introduction about the nature of self-assessment, giving students guided and independent practice in carrying out their own self-assessments, and using formative assessment along the way to see if any en-route instructional adjustments are in order.

The most important element of this third choice-point stems from the teacher's need to recognize that students require support if they are to arrive at reasonably on-target estimates about how well they understand something. It is not as if this sort of ability is conveniently nestled in every student's cognitive arsenal, just waiting to be deployed. Teachers who want to successfully employ this application of formative assessment need to ask themselves this question: *"How can I help my students improve their ability to accurately identify their personal levels of understanding?"*

Choice-Point 4: When to Make An Instructional Adjustment

Even when students are self-reporting their own understanding, the teacher still needs to decide in advance what levels of student-reported understanding will trigger an instructional adjustment.

As noted in Chapter 3, these adjustment triggers should reflect the importance of whatever is being addressed in class. The more significant a building block is to the mastery of the target curricular aim, the less student confusion a teacher should be willing to accept. To illustrate, for a truly pivotal building block—a "must master at all costs" one—a teacher might decide that if more than 10 percent of the students display either yellow or red signals, an instructional adjustment is in order. For a less-important building block, this same teacher might tolerate up to 20 or 30 percent yellow or red signals before instituting an adjustment. As always, the formative assessment process calls for the teacher to decide carefully, in advance of instruction, what levels of adjustment triggers apply to different parts of a lesson.

Choice-Point 5: What Kind of Instructional Adjustment to Make

As a strain of immediate-adjustment formative assessment, this particular application also requires teachers to have an instructional Plan B ready to implement instantly. And, because this application of formative assessment is often used in connection with teachers' explanations, when student's self-reports indicate they are having trouble understanding what's being explained, the most likely adjustment for a teacher to make is to *explain it again differently*.

In practice, this means teachers must be well prepared, having first thought through the chief features of their intended explanations and then asking a question such as, *"If this explanation doesn't do the job, what alternative explanation can I use as a backup?"* Remember, we're talking about making immediate instructional adjustments here—an action that can be undertaken in the twinkling of an eye or, at most, in two twinklings.

Let's be honest. Even splendid instructional adjustments, made instantly and with consummate finesse, will not always work for every student who is having trouble. What are teachers to do when a second round of signaling, conducted *after* an instructional adjustment has been made, reveals there are particular students who still do not understand the subject matter? Well, insofar as it is possible, this is the point at which skillful teachers consider an array of differentiated instructional options, such as the use of peer tutors, specialized subgroup work, involving parents in an at-home support activity, and so on. *How* to provide the extra help is less at issue than *how to find the time and energy* to supply such help. Teachers who use formative assessment are not exempt from the guilt apt to be experienced by teachers facing a flock of diverse learners who learn different things in different ways and at different speeds.

Lest I be accused of proposing the pedagogically impossible, I want to be straight about the issue of instructional differentiation and how it fits into *any* application of the formative assessment process. Because formative assessment is predicated on the frequent collection of assessment evidence regarding students' status, this evidence will often function as an in-your-face message to teachers, who can sometimes fool themselves into thinking all of their students are merrily moving forward. The use of formative assessment splashes cold water on such instructional fantasies. Some students really are not getting what's being taught.

However, suggesting that instructional differentiation will cure this calamity completely is, in my view, downright disingenuous. Differentiated instruction can't solve the problem of students' heterogeneity, but it can help teachers address it. And because formative assessment will toss the differentiation dilemma into a teacher's lap almost every time students are assessed, or any time they signal their levels of understanding, teachers who employ formative assessment will face this issue more frequently than other teachers. If you plan to employ formative assessment, you'll need to get ready for this challenge. I suggest that, given what's practical, you supply as much differentiated instruction as you can. But sleep guiltless at night if you can't cure all learning ills.

Choice-Point 6: How to Help Students More Honestly Report Their Understanding

In this application of formative assessment, teachers are relying on students to provide "good data"—to be candid when reporting whether they are "getting it" or not. There are a host of reasons why students may be reluctant to reveal that they are having difficulty comprehending what's going on in class. Every teacher knows that students can be embarrassed by their ignorance, and that classrooms can be cauldrons of competitiveness, with the more accomplished students wanting to shine and the less-accomplished ones yearning to be invisible. It's to be expected, then, that a teacher looking to use self-reports of understanding as assessment evidence will want to think carefully about how to encourage students to believe it's perfectly OK to reveal that there's something they simply don't understand.

One straightforward approach to this issue is for teachers to reveal, matching candor for candor, that the target outcome for all education is for students *to learn*—and learning does not always occur instantly. What ultimately matters is what students know and can do at the *end* of instruction, not at its beginning or in the middle of it. And successful end-of-instruction learning, the only kind that makes any difference, is more likely to occur when all students let the teacher know when they are having difficulty understanding what's going on *during instruction*, so the teacher can make the instruction better.

It is also useful for teachers to personally shoulder a big lump of responsibility for students' learning. At least some of the time, students' failure to learn is not their failing but the failing of a teacher who has not taught well. Students need to know this. It is easier to say, "I don't understand" when the person who is supposed to help you understand is willing to say, "It's mostly my fault that you don't."

Looking back, then, at the six choices to be faced by any teacher who wishes to make immediate instructional adjustments based on students' self-reported levels of understanding, it should be apparent that teachers can employ a number of variations of this process. Remember, though, that most students will find this application of formative assessment genuinely different from what they ordinarily encounter in school in that *they are being called upon* to help the teacher provide better instruction.

Let's turn, now, to a fictional teacher who uses this application of formative assessment in class, and to an interview with that teacher regarding key decisions the teacher was obliged to make.

In the Classroom

Hector Ramirez teaches English at Foster School, a middle school in a fairly affluent Midwest community. A high percentage of the school's students are Hispanic—most of them second-generation citizens—and have been educated in one of three elementary feeder schools in the district. Hector has taught at Foster School for almost a decade, and in the last two years he has become a strong proponent of formative assessment. One of his school district's regular reports to the public featured a description of Hector's instructional approach. He was chosen chiefly because he frequently employs a variation of formative assessment in which his students supply signals to him indicating how well they understand what's being taught in class and he modifies his instruction as necessary, based on students' self-reported understandings.

A few days after the report was issued, the features editor of the local newspaper, *The Clarion*, arranged for a reporter, Lucy Lacey, to visit Foster School for the purpose of observing Hector's methods in action and conducting an interview.

Key Classroom Events

As Lucy sat down in the back of the 8th grade English class, she noticed that one of the first things students did after sitting down at their desks was to take out three plastic-laminated 3-by 5-inch cards: one red, one yellow, and one green. All students placed the red card on their desk, set the yellow card on top of it, and put the green card on the very top of the stack. The class session was focused on grammar, and as it progressed, Lucy saw different students changing the order of their card stacks so that sometimes the yellow card was on top and sometimes the red card was. Whenever there was a preponderance of yellow or red cards on the top of students' card stacks, Hector would say something such as, "Let's dig into that idea again from a different perspective." At that point, Hector would re-explain what he had explained earlier, doing so in a different way and sharing different examples. As he concluded these second explanations, Lucy saw that many students—but not all—replaced their top yellow or red card with their green card.

In Lucy's opinion, all but two students—George and Joseph—seemed to take the ongoing card-signaling activity seriously. These two boys giggled at one another's card choices and the card choices of the students around them. On two occasions, Hector had to ask George and Joseph to settle down.

This sort of instructional pattern, with Hector explaining and re-explaining certain topics, such as the kinds of pronouns to be used when modifying gerunds, continued until there were just 15 minutes of class time left. At that point, Hector told his students to put away their color-cards and start working on a set of 25 exercises about the appropriate use of gerunds and participles. He distributed the assignment and noted that any of the exercises not completed in class should be completed for homework.

The Interview of Hector Ramirez

by Lucy Lacey

Mr. Ramirez, I really want to thank you for letting me observe your class and for taking time away from your planning period to let me interview you. I found what you were doing quite fascinating, and I think readers of The Clarion *will find it as interesting as I did. I want to ask you particularly about the colored-card system you employed. Is this what educators mean when they talk about "formative assessment"?*

Yes, it's an aspect of it, but if you want your readers to know what's really involved in formative assessment, they'll need to understand that formative assessment is a process—a process in which teachers use assessment evidence to make adjustments in what we are doing. In some instances, assessment evidence is collected through standard kinds of classroom tests. But, as you saw, much of the time in my classes I rely on the use of students' self-reported levels of understanding. In formative assessment, teachers—and sometimes students themselves—use whatever assessment evidence that's collected to make adjustments in what they are doing.

My students' use of color-cards is one way for me to collect evidence of how well they are learning what they are supposed to be learning. Basing subsequent instructional decisions on assessment-elicited evidence is what makes formative assessment distinctive.

I see what you mean, but I noticed that you had your students put away their color-cards during the last segment of the class session. Do you only use it at certain times in a class?

That's an interesting question. Some teachers collect evidence of students' levels of understanding practically all of the time, but I like to do so in only two situations: when I am trying to explain something brand-new to my students and when I am trying to clarify the intended curricular outcomes for a fairly lengthy segment of instruction. These are the times in my unit plans when I'm responsible for presenting information very, very clearly. When the kids indicate they don't understand something, this tells me I haven't succeeded. I need to circle back and offer them a different bite out of the expository apple.

I have a guess as to what the three colored cards indicate. Is it something along the lines of traffic lights?

That's pretty much it, Ms. Lacey. A green card means, "I understand what's going on, and I understand it so well that I can explain it to another student." A yellow card means, "I am pretty certain I understand most of what's going on, but I am not completely certain I understand it all." And a red card means, "I am really confused about what's going on."

I occasionally call on a green-card student to explain something to the rest of the class. It's a way of checking in to be sure that "green carders" do understand things as well as they claim to, and it also discourages students from leaving green cards on top of their stacks if they don't really comprehend a concept.

I saw you scanning the classroom quite often, and I assume it was to determine how many cards of different colors were on top of students' card stacks. What do you do with this information?

Did you notice that whenever there were lots of yellow or red cards on top, I went back and re-explained a point? Well, my rule of thumb is that whenever what I'm explaining is very important, if about one-third of the students are showing yellow or red cards, I re-explain. For less-important topics, I re-explain when half or more of the students have yellow or red cards on top. Of course, the proportion of red cards to yellow cards also makes a difference. When I see what I think of as "the Red Sea" out there, I know for certain that it's time to haul out another explanation.

I'm thinking about a part of the lesson when you were explaining the kinds of pronouns to use when modifying gerunds. As I watched what was going on, you seemed to re-explain that concept twice, and you provided lots and lots of examples. Why?

I'm glad you spotted that, Ms. Lacey. I did this because first re-explanation seemed to fall flat—almost flatter than the initial one! How did I know this? Well, very few of the red-card kids or yellow-card kids changed their cards to green while I was talking. Now, I personally thought my re-explanation was clear, but based on my scan of students' top cards, they didn't agree. So I had a third go at it, with lots more examples. And this seemed to do the trick.

Right. At that point, I noticed most of students moved a green card to the top of their stacks. But backtracking, if you had not been using your signaling system, you simply would not have known that students weren't getting your second re-explanation—or your first re-explanation, for that matter.

Exactly. I'd have had no idea. Like I said, I thought I'd done a good job, and if I hadn't seen evidence to contrary, I'd have gone on thinking that until the end of the unit—right up until I saw a set of mystifyingly low test scores. That's one of the big reasons formative assessment is so worthwhile. It lets teachers know—based on real evidence from students—what instruction works and what instruction doesn't. Are there any other questions I can answer for you?

Well, Mr. Ramirez, I don't want to sound critical, but I couldn't help noticing those two boys over on the left side of the class—Joseph and George. They didn't seem to take what was going on very seriously. In fact, at several points during the class session, they seemed to be making fun of the color-card use. What's the story with those two? Do you sometimes get students who just don't go along with this approach?

Oh, yes, Joseph and George. The thing to remember, Ms. Lacey, is that very few kids have any experience in classes like mine. I'm enlisting my students as allies who can help improve my instruction, which can improve their learning. For each new group of students I work with, it takes maybe a month before they really begin to understand what they are being asked to do. Joseph and George are both transfer students, and they've only been at Foster School for a little over two weeks. I'm sure they'll get it, but this will come less from my telling them how they should conduct themselves during our color-card sessions and more—far more—from watching how the other students behave during those sessions.

Also, every month or so, I try to build in at least one activity I refer to as a "recalibration drill." It is an effort to help students be as accurate as they can when judging the degree to which they understand what's going on in class. These recalibration drills are especially useful for students like Joseph and George, who haven't had much experience in judging whether they understand something or not.

And how do these recalibration drills work?

Most of them revolve around students' confidential—not public—estimates of how well they understand the topic I've been explaining. Usually they write down a number from 1 to 10, with the number meant to coincide roughly with how well they believe they understand the material. An 8 to 10 represents "green-level" understanding; a 5 to 7 represents "yellow-level" understanding, and a 4 or below signifies "red-level" understanding which, as you've seen, is really no understanding at all.

Then I administer a brief, 10-item test of some sort. I read out the answers, and the students correct their own papers so that they can see how close their estimated level of understanding was to their test-demonstrated level of understanding. Although I'm careful to point out that testing isn't a super-precise enterprise, I also explain that if their estimated and tested levels of understanding are off by more than three or four points, they should try to sharpen the accuracy of their estimates. At no point do students reveal either their estimates or their test scores to me. The whole purpose of this activity is to increase the accuracy of students' judgments about how well they understand what's taking place in class.

I noticed a few of students—those two girls near the windows— seemed to have a red card on top of their pile almost constantly. What can you do about such students? Surely you can't keep adjusting your instruction until every single student reports understanding what's being taught?

With that question you get at one of the most troubling parts of the instructional process. In our district, just this academic year, there has been a big push toward "effective differentiation" when we teach. Well, there's not a teacher I know who wants to see children left behind, and we do the best we can to address everybody's needs. Whenever a subset of my students just seem unable to catch on—like Marisa and Daniela, the girls you noticed, as well as Cris and Carlos over on the other side of the room—I try to find a time during the period when I can get the rest of the class working on an activity and then pull those red-card kids into a small group where I can re-address whatever topic has been giving them trouble. During that small-group re-explanation, I sometimes ask a "green-card kid" to be my assistant and sit in while I try to re-explain for the red-carders. Then, after I ask as many questions as I can, my "assistant" continues working with the group while I return to the remaining students. It's not a perfect system, but it often seems to do the job for those students who are having difficulties.

An Interview Look-Back

Here are my three take-aways from Lucy Lacey's interview with Hector Ramirez.

First, there was Hector's choice about when to use the color-card signal system. He apparently only uses it in two situations: (1) when he is trying to explain new things to his class, and (2) when he is trying to help students understand where they are headed at the outset of a new instructional sequence. Promoting students' clarified understandings about where they are headed instructionally is so very important to all instructional approaches, and this strikes me as an excellent time for Hector to use his system. The choice of when to use this particular variant of formative assessment, or to use it at all, is one that each teacher must make.

A second consideration worth some attention were the adjustment triggers Hector had established for his "more-important" and "less-important" content. Because most formative assessment applications based on students' self-reported levels of understanding will require teachers to make really quick adjustment decisions, his use of fairly general levels (one-third of the class for certain topics or one-half of the class for other topics) makes a good deal of sense. The nature of the instructional adjustments in this instance always involved a second explanation—and in one case, a third explanation. That Hector was ready with these adjustments is a sign of proper planning and effective application.

Finally, the presence of the two recent transfer students, Joseph and George, reminds us that the application of formative assessment treated in this chapter represents a dramatic change for most students—one that may require time, practice, and patience.

Reflection Questions

1. If you were a teacher tasked with making your students more accurate self-assessors, how would you go about it? What procedures would you employ?

2. If you were trying explain how to deploy differentiated instruction to address the needs of struggling students to a group of seasoned teachers, what would your advice be?

3. Of the six choice-points identified for this application of formative assessment, which one do you think would be the easiest for a teacher to make a decision about? Which one would be the most difficult? How might a teacher go about making the most difficult choice more easily?

4. Think about how you might employ this application of formative assessment with one of your current units of instruction. Consider all the choice-points outlined in this chapter.

5

Near-Future Instructional Adjustments

I don't drink coffee, but most of my friends do, and I've yet to hear a single one of them praise the merits of instant coffee over a cup that's been slowly brewed. Not everything in life needs to be instant. Sometimes, slow-brewing is a better bet. And so it is with the application of formative assessment we'll examine in this chapter.

In the preceding two chapters, we saw that there are points in the instructional process when immediate instructional adjustments are the best choice. Many of those "must-make-now" changes are a response to a critical misunderstanding or a misapplication of a subskill—the kind of student errors that, if not corrected pronto, may linger and muck up the course of learning. In those instances it makes perfect sense for teachers to prepare, and then provide, an on-the-spot change in what's going on instructionally. In other circumstances, however, it makes more sense for teachers to take a few days to mull over how best to modify their instructional plans in order to increase the odds that whatever adjustment they make will successfully enhance students' learning.

Implementation Considerations

No hard and fast rules exist regarding which student shortcomings must be addressed by immediate adjustments versus near-future adjustments. But, in general, the near-future instructional adjustments will usually involve more lengthy instructional activities focused on remedying more substantial student deficits—things that can't be addressed with a very quick fix or a simple redirection. These kinds of challenges are often encountered when the content is more complex. To put it in "learning progression terms," this application of formative assessment is well suited to occasions when a teacher is focusing on a subskill-sort of building block containing several subcomponents—perhaps a subskill that depends on a student's satisfying three distinct evaluative criteria.

When teachers are tackling building blocks containing two or more subcomponents, the near-future approach permits the creation of *efficient* and truly *tailored* instructional adjustments. The temporal interval between evidence collection and adjustment implementation gives a teacher time to target any instructional changes at students' diagnostically assessed weaknesses. If the assessment itself is thoughtfully prepared to focus on particular aspects of the subskill or enabling knowledge in question, the teacher will have great information to go on.

To illustrate, let's say I'm a science teacher teaching a six-week instructional unit on designing and implementing randomized control-group scientific experiments. I want to assess my students' mastery of the second of three building blocks in the unit's learning progression. As part of my instructional planning, I've identified three subcomponents of this second building block—two subskills and one body of enabling knowledge. Given that there are three things students need to learn in order to master this second building block, I've decided to build a paper-and-pencil assessment to help me figure out which of the three components students are having trouble mastering. So I give the test, and, when I look at the results, I can see that my students have done well on two of the three subcomponents but seem to be completely lost with respect to the remaining one. With this information, I will be able to devise an instructional adjustment truly suitable for dealing with the specific subcomponent that's causing students trouble.

And let's not forget that this application of formative assessment may allow a teacher to skip the adjustment preparation entirely. Although the teacher does need to think generally about what Plans B, C, and D might be, there's no need to work out the specifics of those plans in advance, as would be required for the immediate-adjustment version of formative assessment. Instead, the teacher works out Plan B only when the evidence indicates that it is necessary, and can then tailor it to real, evidence-supported needs. This translates to time saved and burnout avoided.

This Application's Key Choice-Points

As with all applications of formative assessment, near-future adjustment presents a set of choices for any teacher preparing to use it (see Figure 5.1). You'll notice that several of these decisions mirror those previously discussed in relation to a teacher's immediate instructional adjustments; although we'll touch on those already treated choice-points briefly, we'll give most of our attention here to the new considerations.

Choice-Point 1: Whether Instructional Adjustment Is Feasible During This Part of the Lesson or Unit

This application of formative assessment allows teachers to (1) assess their students, (2) discover if an instructional adjustment is needed, and (3) install an instructional modification a day or so after the assessment. For this application to be carried out, teachers need to be sure that *if* the assessment evidence indicates it's adjustment time, then a potentially effective adjustment will be available. It could be something as simple as providing a new explanation with different examples and resources or as complex as a new assignment designed to provide additional scaffolding to support subskill development. Whatever the adjustment is, the teacher needs to be able to put it into play in short order.

FIGURE 5.1

Six Choice-Points for Using Formative Assessment to Make a Near-Future Instructional Adjustment

1. **Whether instructional adjustment is feasible during this part of the lesson or unit.** Are potential instructional adjustments on hand? If not, can one be created quickly enough?

2. **Which assessment to use.** Which assessment techniques will be employed to measure students' current status?

3. **When to collect assessment evidence.** How should assessment evidence be collected from students? At which points in the lesson or unit?

4. **How to design the assessment for maximum diagnostic value.** For each subskill or body of knowledge being assessed, how many test items are necessary to support valid conclusions about students' status?

5. **What level of performance will trigger an instructional adjustment.** How poorly should students perform for a near-future instructional adjustment to be made?

6. **What adjustments to make and when.** If students' performances dictate an instructional adjustment must be made, what should it be, and when should it be made?

For instance, if the assessment evidence indicates students need more practice in classifying objects according to a subtle, three-category classification scheme, will a teacher who has no on-the-shelf exercises really have sufficient time to generate a set of classification exercises for students? If whatever's needed to implement an instructional adjustment is not already at hand or cannot be created soon enough, then this application of the formative assessment process is—in such an instance—inappropriate.

For the teacher, then, the first question to ask is, *"What kind of difficulties do I anticipate my students having with this material?"* It can be very helpful to review the learning progression at this point, focusing on the specific building block that's the target of current or upcoming instruction and that building block's subcomponents. In answering this question, the teacher should consider past experience with this material, as well as the particular strengths and weaknesses of this year's class. Are the students likely to hit snags that can be untangled quickly and easily? Or is sorting out the problem likely to require more significant amounts of time and more substantial effort? In the former case, the teacher might do well to consider an immediate adjustment instead. In the latter case, the teacher must ask another question: *"If I don't already have a likely instructional adjustment ready to roll, can I create one within a day or two, based on the assessment evidence I get?"* If the answer here is yes, this brand of formative assessment is a solid choice.

Choice-Point 2: Which Assessment to Use

In all applications of the formative assessment process, teachers need to decide what sorts of assessment devices will most efficiently supply the evidence they need to make valid inferences about their students' current knowledge and skill levels. In some instances, as we saw in Chapter 4, teachers can rely on their students' self-reported levels of understanding for this purpose. In other cases, teachers may choose more traditional kinds of assessment approaches, such as selected-response or constructed-response test items.

The dominant determinant of how best to assess students' status will always be the nature of the knowledge or subskill to be assessed, and the question the teacher needs to ask is, *"Will the assessment approach I am considering supply me with evidence that allows me to accurately determine what my students can and can't do relative to this subskill or body of knowledge?"*

Note the specificity: Teachers want to choose an assessment that can tell them which aspects of the content their students are and are not mastering. Thoughtfully constructed multiple-choice tests are excellent tools here, especially when the teacher designs them to target the various instructionally addressable subcomponents of the building block in question. (We'll talk further about this in the discussion of Choice-Point 4, beginning on page 92.) Constructed-response assessments, if carefully created, can also be quite illuminating to the teacher. Students can reveal, based on their short answers or extended essay responses, where they're confused.

If the content in question focuses exclusively on only one skill or one body of knowledge—and there are no significant subcomponents nestled within it—the assessment tactic known as "exit tickets" or "tickets out the door" is a good choice. You may be familiar with this technique. Early in a class session, the teacher poses a central question to students related to the "big idea" of that day's lesson. In an English course, for example, such a question might be "Why are concrete details so important in good writing?" Then, after the lesson, as students are exiting the classroom, they supply the teacher or a designated student with a card or a slip of paper on which they've written their name and their answer to the day's question. The teacher can survey the students' responses and use the resultant insights to decide if a near-future instructional adjustment is in order and what that adjustment might be.

Choice-Point 3: When to Collect Assessment Evidence

My general advice on this matter, offered in *TA1,* is unchanged. I believe teachers should build "lean" learning progressions—with fewer building blocks rather than more—and then, *at a minimum,* assess students' mastery of each building block in the progression. These assessments are best scheduled to take place toward the end of the instructional period the teacher has allotted for a particular building block, at a point when there is still time to make an instructional adjustment, if such an adjustment is necessary.

As before, I include the "at a minimum" to recognize that a teacher may also choose to measure students' mastery of a variety of subskills or bodies of knowledge—subcomponents of the building blocks in the learning progression or other things that the teacher may want students to learn during a unit that are not necessarily essential to achieving the target curricular aim. Remember that the key variable in the "when to assess" question is a teacher's inclination to make instructional adjustments. The question to ask is, "*At this particular point in my instructional plan, am I willing to take*

the time to gather assessment evidence, analyze it for the purpose of
making an instructional adjustment, and make that adjustment if
it is necessary?" If the answer is yes, that's the time to collect assessment evidence.

And what about pre-assessment? Does a teacher's use of an assessment before instruction gets under way—say, at the start of a school year or before kicking off an instructional unit—mean the teacher is using formative assessment? Does tweaking one's instructional plans for a unit based on pre-assessment data count as a near-future instructional adjustment? I believe the answer to these questions is no, and that's coming from someone who has been touting the virtues of pre-assessment for nearly a half a century.

When I joined the faculty of the UCLA Graduate School of Education in 1962, one of the instructional maxims I pitched to my would-be teachers was that they should routinely pre-assess their students, definitely at the outset of a school year and often at the beginning of any sort of multi-week instruction unit, in order to make sure they didn't teach kids to do things those kids already knew how to do and ensure that kids possessed the entry skills and knowledge to pursue the teacher's chosen instructional objectives. Pre-assessment was then, and is now, a wonderful way of (1) avoiding redundant instruction and (2) assuring that students are properly positioned to learn the stuff a teacher plans to teach. But, by definition, pre-assessment takes place *before* teaching is under way—that's where the "pre" comes in. So while pre-assessment is most certainly a good thing for teachers to do, it isn't really part of the formative assessment festival. To put it another way, when a teacher is considering when to collect assessment evidence for the purpose of making a near-future instructional adjustment, that teacher should concentrate on the instructional period itself.

Choice-Point 4: How to Design the Assessment for Maximum Diagnostic Value

When the goal is to assess students' mastery of complex material and figure out explicitly what it is that students can or can't do for the purpose of informing a targeted, near-future instructional adjustment, a teacher will typically want to turn to longer paper-and-pencil tests and figure out how best to use them to tease out useful information.

One strength of the near-future adjustment application of formative assessment is that it gives teachers time to tailor an instructional response to the specific areas of students' struggle. If the building block in question contains two subcomponent subskills, for example, and it's Subcomponent 2 that students have not mastered, the teacher's instructional adjustment might be an additional, scaffolded practice activity focused on Subcomponent 2. The key is to design an assessment that can provide this degree of measurement detail. There must be a sufficient number of items per assessed subcomponent so the teacher can get a fairly accurate fix on exactly what it is that students can or can't do.

Again, there are no set rules regarding how many items—multiple-choice or otherwise—this kind of fix-getting requires; it depends on the grain size of the skills or knowledge involved. The larger the grain size—meaning, the broader the body of knowledge or the more cognitively demanding the skill—the more items will be needed. I'm happy to say, though, that all the teacher really has to do is pose the following question: *"For this particular skill (or body of knowledge), how many item responses do I think I'll need to arrive at a defensible inference about my students' mastery level?"* If the teacher believes a particular collection of items is large enough to support a sound decision to adjust or not adjust instruction, then it probably is. More information on measurement issues, such as how many items to use when arriving at valid test-based inferences about students, can be found in many classroom assessment textbooks (e.g., Popham, 2011).

Choice-Point 5: What Level of Performance Will Trigger an Instructional Adjustment

This application's fifth choice-point is identical to its counterpart in the previous two chapters. Again, the two-part question for the teacher to ask is, *"What is the cutoff point for an acceptable individual student performance, and how many students in the class must fall below that performance level for me to conclude that an instructional adjustment is necessary?"* What's crucial with this fifth choice-point is that *it must be done,* and it will usually be done *better* if it is considered in advance rather than when the assessment data have already been collected.

In the near-future adjustments application of formative assessment, a teacher does have the luxury of looking over students' actual performances before arriving at an adjust/don't adjust decision. This choice will always be a judgment call, but having time to mull over the assessment evidence can lead to more insightful decisions.

Choice-Point 6: What Adjustments to Make and When

Making adjustments is more difficult than it might seem. When assessment evidence indicates that an instructional adjustment is needed—either a change in what a teacher is doing now or planning to do soon—often it's not instantly obvious what needs to be done differently. Most teachers have internalized guidelines on how to create sensible lesson plans and how to craft longer-duration instructional sequences, but preservice and in-service training typically devotes less attention to what to do when those sensible plans and sequences don't pan out.

The most fundamental instructional adjustments boil down to a teacher's reteaching something in a different manner. Back on page 58, Figure 3.2 presented a set of potential adjustment tactics that teachers could consider. These possibilities are applicable to any near-future instructional adjustments. The several days teachers might allot for analyzing the assessment data, figuring out an appropriate response, and preparing any associated classroom activities can be a distinct advantage. Of course, teachers have more to do each day than massage their intended instructional activities, and the often overwhelming nature of those other commitments can get in the way of lighting on a magnificent massaging move. Often, it's about doing the best possible job with the time, resources, and energy available.

Generally speaking, the sooner an adjustment can be made, the better. But it is clearly wiser for the teacher to take a day or two to come up with a *winning* instructional adjustment than it would be to install an early, ineffective adjustment. A teacher should consider the benefits associated with addressing learning problems quickly and the likely effectiveness of whatever adjustment the teacher has in mind.

Having looked at the most prominent choice-points faced by teachers who choose to employ a near-future adjustments application of formative assessment, let's see how a fictional teacher might actually tackle this sort of application. As in past chapters, you should be directing your attention to the decisions our fictional teacher makes as she uses this version of formative assessment.

In the Classroom

Olivia Adams teaches 5th graders in a western state. This is Olivia's sixth year as a teacher, and all of those years have been spent at Baker Elementary, where she has taught both 4th and 5th grade. She and her colleagues are ardent supporters of formative assessment, which they first learned about three years ago while taking part in a yearlong, district-sponsored professional learning community.

Their use of formative assessment is of great interest to teacher education students from the nearly state college. With arrangements coordinated by their professor, Bill James, these teachers-in-training typically arrive in small teams of three or four students to observe a week's worth of instruction given by Baker Elementary teachers. Afterward, they write up comments and questions in an "Instructional Highlights Report," which they submit to their professor.

Key Classroom Events

Excerpts from the Instructional Highlights Report Submitted to Professor James by Student Observer Team K

Our team had the pleasure of observing a fabulous 5th grade teacher, Olivia Adams. Although all three of us profited immensely from watching how Mrs. Adams carried out her instruction, as directed by this assignment, the instructional highlights we are reporting on here focus principally on Mrs. Adams's use of formative assessment.

During a brief pre-school conversation with Mrs. Adams on the Monday of the week of our observation, she informed us that she often uses formative assessment to deal with more immediate student misunderstandings, and students have become familiar with using sets of letter-cards to supply answers to prepared multiple-choice questions. Mrs. Adams uses the performance data she collects in this way to inform what she calls "immediate instructional adjustments." However, she let us know that the instance of formative assessment we would be observing would be something else: a classroom test, the data from which she would use to inform a "near-future instructional adjustment."

During our Monday meeting with Mrs. Adams, she shared her lesson plans for the week, explaining that her language arts instruction would wrap up a focus on two new statewide content standards in reading, both of which dealt with the use of reference tools: *"Students will be able to decide which reference tool to employ when searching for particular kinds of information,"* and *"Students, having selected an appropriate reference tool to use, will be able to employ this tool properly."* She showed us the classroom test (about 20 items, some multiple-choice, some short-answer) that she would administer Monday as a way of "checking in" on students' emerging mastery of these standards. Based on the test data, Mrs. Adams explained to us, she might need to adjust her instructional plans for the remainder of the week.

As it turned out, her students' performances on the Monday test did lead to an instructional adjustment. On Tuesday, Mrs. Adams informed her students that she had reviewed the test results and would be supplying several new instructional ideas during the next several days' classes. When she returned students' test papers to them, we noted that the papers had corrections, but none bore a grade letter. We later confirmed with Mrs. Adams that these tests were evaluated but ungraded.

During Wednesday's reading class, Mrs. Adams spent about 10 minutes reviewing each of five specific reference tools she wanted her students to become adept at using: (1) a thesaurus, (2) a dictionary, (3) a book index, (4) a table of contents, and (5) an Internet search engine. She "re-explained" the use of each of these tools, apparently somewhat differently than she had explained them during the previous week. For each reference tool discussed, Mrs. Adams presented clear, step-by-step directions regarding its use. She spent more time on how to use an Internet search engine because, as she explained to her students, "this was the part of Monday's test that gave lots of us trouble." As the Wednesday instruction was coming to an end, Mrs. Adams distributed a set of take-home practice exercises, accompanied by an answer key. Students were to submit their completed homework exercises on Friday morning, and almost every student did.

On Friday, Mrs. Adams conducted a rather freewheeling Q&A session in which she would post a question about how to use a specific reference tool, and then call on one student to answer this question. During this questioning period, she employed an interesting student-identification technique wherein she randomly selected a popsicle stick from a full cup of them. Each stick had a student's name written on it in magic marker. Mrs. Adams would ask a question, draw a "name stick," and call on that randomly selected student to provide an answer. (Students were very alert and engaged throughout this Q&A segment.) Near the end of Friday's reading instruction, Mrs. Adams read aloud a set of about a dozen True/False questions, each question dealing with the use of one of the reference tools. All students, on her command, signified a True or False answer to each question by holding their thumbs up or down in front of their chests. At the end of this brief thumbs-up/down quiz, Mrs. Adams complimented her students for doing a great job in learning how to use reference tools.

Respectfully submitted,

Joseph Givens, Alice Avery, and Coretta Green
(Observer Team K)

The Interview of Olivia Adams

by Professor Bill James

Olivia, thanks so much for giving me a chunk of your afternoon. I know how busy you must be, and I really appreciate it. I also appreciate your letting the college's teacher education students regularly sit in on your classes. The students in our program learn so much from watching teachers like you and your colleagues here at Baker.

It's a real pleasure for us to do it, Bill. The observers we get from your classes are so polite and so *quiet* that it's sometimes hard to tell they are even there. This last group—the ones who watched my class last week, were especially silent—almost invisible. Do you folks at the college give them stealth training?

I'm pleased to hear that. Having three adults observe a class of 4th graders without being intrusive is quite impressive. I'll let them know. I hope they confirmed what I recently told you on the phone—that I'm really eager to learn more about the formative assessment process. And everyone at Baker says you really know how to make it work. Can I ask you some questions about what went on last week? I'll base my inquiries on a written summary the three observers submitted yesterday about what they saw going on in your class. All right if I proceed?

Sure, roar ahead, Bill. I hope my answers will help you get a good handle on formative assessment. All of us here at Baker Elementary School think it's a marvelous process, and we'd love to see young teachers emerge from your college's teacher-prep program ready to use it in their own classrooms.

Well, based on the observer team's report, it seems that the test you gave last Monday got things under way. What can you tell me about that test?

Right, that test was the start. I put a lot of thinking and planning into it. You may already know this, but the State Board of Education recently changed our content standards for reading. Two of the new standards focus on first selecting and then using appropriate reference tools. When I was putting this unit together, I went ahead and built a test that would help me determine which—if either—of those two new content standards needed more or different instructional attention. As I've said, this is the first time I'm explicitly teaching these skills to my kids; I made a plan for how to do it, but I knew I wanted to check in about midway through that plan and see how effective my lessons had been.

I suppose that you devoted some questions on your Monday test to the "choosing a reference tool" skill and some questions to the "using a reference tool" skill. How did you decide on the number of items to include for each of those two skills?

It's always a puzzle when you are putting together a test to measure students' mastery of different things. The two reading skills we're talking about are related, but they definitely call for different kinds of cognitive operations on the part of students. For the first skill, students need to figure out which of five possible tools is suitable for a specific task. For the second skill, students need to know how each of the tools can be used to do its job. So these are different sorts of skills. What I decided to do was to create a 20-item test in which there would be five items measuring the Choosing Skill and 15 items measuring the Using Skill—with three of those 15 items devoted to each of the five reference tools we are supposed to get our students to master.

Do I think I made the right decision regarding a suitable number of items? I *think* I did. I thought five questions for Choosing was plenty—one question for each of the reference tools. Honestly, I don't think most students will really have too much trouble choosing among those diverse research tools—once students understand the different function of each tool, I mean. But the actual usage of certain of the five reference tools is pretty tricky, so I figured I should have at least three questions for each of those. Oh, and I will add that I talked over the item-number issue with the other two 5th grade teachers here at Baker to see what they thought. Both said my decisions seemed sound to them.

The idea behind this test administration, I assume, is that if the data the test returned showed your students had not mastered one or both of those two reference-usage skills, you would do something to address the problem. Is that right?

That's exactly right. One of the interesting features of this kind of near-future application of formative assessment is that when you discover you need to alter your originally planned instructional activities, you have a few days to come up with these new plans. And that's what happened here.

Could you tell me more about that process?

Sure. Well, Monday's test results showed me that almost all of my students were quite capable when it came to the Choosing Skill. Twenty-three of my 26 kids—or about 90 percent—got all five of those questions right. But my students were significantly weaker at the Using Skill. This meant I needed to adjust my instructional plans. Originally we were going to move ahead to another content standard altogether, one dealing with students' skills when reading expository materials. But I could see that they needed more time to work on the Using Skill. Actually, to be precise, my students did very well on test items focused on using an index and a table of contents. There were few, if any, mistakes on those items. Where the kids fell short was in answering questions about using a dictionary, a thesaurus, and especially an Internet search engine. More than half of the class missed two out of the three questions associated with using each of those tools.

What I needed to do was put together a new, hopefully more successful treatment of how to use a dictionary, a thesaurus, and an online search engine. In past years, my instruction has tended to suffer from insufficient time on task—that is, I've tended not to give my students enough time to practice new skills before moving on to the next item on my instructional agenda. So my first thought, when it came to making an instructional adjustment in this case, was to give the kids more practice activities. I also wondered about how effectively I had modeled how to use those three tools. Maybe I needed to talk through the process with the kids a bit more? I assume the observer team told you what went on in class later during the rest of the week?

Yes, the report noted that you came up with a new set of instructional activities focused on using a dictionary, a thesaurus, and an online search engine—the three tools where students' usage skills were weakest.

The planning of those activities took some thought. Remember, this is the first year we've had these particular content standards—and there's such a distinct breakout of the skills related to how students are supposed to use these reference tools. Well, I didn't have any ready-to-use practice exercises in my files. Next year, if I find I need to make an instructional adjustment for this content standard, I'll be able to use or modify the set of activities I worked up for this group of students.

At any rate, my adjustment had three parts. It began with Wednesday's lesson, focused on the Using Skill. I re-explained the three "weak" reference tools from a "how to use them" perspective, presenting different examples than the ones I had used last week. The second part of the adjustment was to have students work on a set of practice activities for Wednesday night's homework. I reviewed students' work and used the evidence I found there to fine-tune Friday's lesson. On Thursday, we did not deal with language arts because of a district-directed compressed-schedule activity, but on Friday, we had a Q&A activity, in which I called on students at random to answer a series of True/False items related to using a dictionary, thesaurus, and a search engine.

I can see how planning for all three activities would have eaten up a good chunk of time. How long can a teacher take to plan these near-future adjustments?"

It really depends on the nature of what's being taught and the magnitude of students' problems with it. When I'm applying formative assessment in this way, I try to make my adjustments no later than three days after collecting the assessment data. You might think the quicker the adjustment, the better, but you also have to take the time to ensure a quality adjustment—to increase the odds that what you do differently this time will make the difference.

Oh, Olivia, could I get to you backtrack a minute to your technique for randomly selecting students for True/False responses during that Q&A session? Was that activity part of the formative assessment process?

Actually, no, it's not. You might think so, but asking students questions one at a time like that gives me assessment information about just that *one* student. To make a valid assessment-based adjustment decision for the whole class, I need to assess all—or almost all—of my students. I love these "pluck-stick" activities, as I call them, because the chance of being called on keeps all the kids plugged in and attentive, but one-at-a-time questioning activities doesn't and shouldn't inform adjustment decisions for the whole class.

I suppose the same reasoning goes for class discussion. You can't have enough students responding to come up with a class-focused estimate of students' status.

That's right, Bill. Class discussions are great, and I use them often. But I don't see them as an activity that yields actionable assessment evidence.

Well, Olivia, I really want to thank you for this session. I learned a great deal regarding what a teacher thinks about when implementing a "near-future adjustments" application of formative assessment. What you've told me will really help me get our prospective teachers ready to use formative assessment themselves. Thanks again.

You're very welcome.

An Interview Look-Back

Two issues emerge from this interview that I think warrant particular consideration.

First, notice how Olivia laid out the rationale for the way she constructed the 20-item assessment she used to determine if an instructional adjustment was necessary. She didn't create an equal number items to measure mastery of the two separate reference-tool skills; instead, she identified which of these two skills was the major one and which the minor one. The minor one was the Choosing Skill, and she allocated just five items to its measurement. The major one was the Using Skill, and she devoted 15 items to assessing students' mastery of it. Because the Using Skill dealt with five separate reference tools, and Olivia needed to gauge students' ability to use each of the tools, she created three items for each of the reference tools.

The second issue to consider is the nature of Olivia's evidence-informed instructional adjustment. The adjustment had three separate parts: Wednesday's re-explanation with new examples, Wednesday's new set of practice activities for homework, and Friday's Q&A session. Do all instructional adjustments need to be this elaborate? No. Instructional adjustment—in type and scope—should always reflect the kind of learning shortcomings the teacher is attempting to ameliorate.

In passing, you might have also noted that Olivia seemed to have had her class accept the idea that some of their tests and homework exercises will not be graded. You may also have noticed that, on Friday, Olivia closed her multi-part instructional adjustment with the kind of thumbs-up/down assessment activity that, as we saw in Chapter 3, can be used to make decisions about immediate instructional adjustments. Because the observer team's report mentioned no immediate instructional alterations during that Friday activity, we can surmise that Olivia's students performed well on that thumbs-up/down assessment, and no further adjustments were necessary.

Reflection Questions

1. What factors should a teacher consider when deciding whether to make on-the-spot instructional adjustments versus waiting a day or so to make an instructional adjustment? In which situations would a teacher be better off scrapping plans for an instant adjustment in order to work up a near-future instructional adjustment?

2. Why is it so important that the assessment evidence collected for a near-future adjustment be genuinely diagnostic?

3. Do you agree or disagree that pre-assessment, although important for a teacher's selection of curricular aims that mesh well with a particular group of students' prior learning and current capabilities, is not technically a part of formative assessment? What is the rationale for your position?

4. Think about how you might employ this application of formative assessment with one of your current units of instruction. Consider all the choice-points discussed in this chapter.

6

Last-Chance
Instructional Adjustments

In professional baseball, recent decades have seen the emergence of a special kind of pitcher called a closer. A closer is a relief pitcher used only during the late stages of a ballgame, perhaps in the eighth or ninth inning of a nine-inning game. The mission of a closer is to "save" a game in which the closer's team is ahead: to make sure the opposing team doesn't score enough runs to catch up or take the lead. Well, there's an application of the formative assessment process that's remarkably similar to the late-inning efforts of a baseball team's closer. It too is restricted to a very specific set of circumstances. It's called a *last-chance instructional adjustment*, and it's undertaken by the teachers who use it as a final way to help students master certain content in the days leading up to a big test.

Implementation Considerations

Remembering that formative assessment works by providing assessment-elicited evidence to teachers (or students) so they can decide whether to change what they are doing, last-chance adjustment application is something teachers should use only when two specific conditions are satisfied. Let's consider both of those "last-chance" circumstances.

The Approach of a Significant Assessment

What the teacher is trying to do with this application of formative assessment is determine how ready students are for the upcoming "big test." If the evidence shows students are *not* performing as well as the teacher had hoped, the teacher can make some last-minute instructional moves in an effort to address areas where students' performances are falling short.

Now, when I say, "big test," what do I mean? I definitely include the kinds of externally imposed "high-stakes" examinations commonly used in the United States in connection with state or federal accountability programs. Typically, students' performances on these tests will have important consequences for them personally (in, say, grade-to-grade promotion) or important consequences for their teachers and school (such as serving as a measure of teacher effectiveness that will factor into compensation or influence the public's perception of a school's quality).

But a "big test" doesn't have to be externally imposed. I know that many teachers create assessments to measure students' mastery of what the teacher sees as particularly significant curricular outcomes. Think, for example, of a middle school English teacher who has been working for almost three months to foster her students' abilities to compose first-rate expository essays. The teacher knows that when her middle-schoolers reach 11th grade, one of the skills they will need to demonstrate on a statewide "diploma denial" test is the ability to write an expository essay. Accordingly, the teacher believes her students' acquisition of this particular essay-writing skill important enough to warrant the use of last-chance formative assessment. Therefore, she'll apply formative assessment in this way before she completes her instructional activities focused on this skill, administers the final exam, and considers her work on this skill-acquisition complete. Here, a big test is not about the kind of accountability that politicians talk about, but about the teacher's being accountable to her students and true to her own instructional priorities.

To sum up, the first necessary condition for using this application of formative assessment is that an important assessment must be looming in the relatively near future, and it can be (1) an externally imposed high-stakes exam or (2) a test of skills or knowledge the teacher regards as particularly significant. If this condition is not satisfied, then a last-chance application of formative assessment is probably not appropriate.

Sufficient Time for an Instructional Response

The last-chance adjustment application of formative assessment makes sense only if, after the assessment's results are available, there will be adequate time for a diagnostically illuminated instructional response. Suppose, for example, that a districtwide mathematics test is coming up at the close of a school year's first semester, and a 5th grade teacher wants his students to shine on that test. The teacher might administer what is often called a *dress rehearsal exam* to his students two weeks before Test Day. This will allow the teacher two weeks' worth of last-minute math instruction to help his students perform well on the actual high-stakes test.

But note that this second condition indicates there is time for "diagnostically illuminated" instruction, not just more time for *more* instruction. The purpose of a dress rehearsal exam is to help the teacher more accurately focus on the skills and knowledge that the assessment evidence shows to be areas of need. If the timing is such that it's impossible to achieve this purpose, then administering the exam doesn't make much sense.

This Application's Key Choice-Points

Teachers contemplating the use of this application of formative assessment will need to consider a number of the choice-points addressed in prior chapters, such as setting adjustment triggers for each skill or body of knowledge being assessed. But there are three decisions that are particularly significant to this rather special, and rather infrequently used, application of formative assessment. Not surprisingly, those decisions, presented in Figure 6.1, correlate with the conditions of its use.

FIGURE 6.1

Three Choce-Points for Using Formative Assessment to Make a Last-Chance Instructional Adjustment

1. **Whether the upcoming assessment is sufficiently significant.** Are an impending assessment's results important enough to warrant the use of this application? Or is students' mastery of the skills and knowledge being assessed by the upcoming test important enough to warrant use of this application?

2. **Whether the upcoming assessment is adequately diagnostic.** Is the planned dress rehearsal exam designed to generate an accurate and detailed picture of students' strengths and weaknesses?

3. **What the potential instructional particulars will be.** When should the dress rehearsal exam be administered to ensure there's enough time for diagnostically targeted instruction? Once the data are in, what instructional adjustments might be made to bring students to mastery?

Choice-Point 1: Whether the Upcoming Assessment Is Sufficiently Significant

Theoretically, last-chance instructional adjustments can be made prior to the administration of just about any test. But developing a dress rehearsal exam and budgeting the time and effort to provide whatever instruction the resulting performance data might dictate require an additional investment on the teacher's part. Is the upcoming test really important enough to make this extra level of assessment worth this time and effort?

For the first kind of big test identified, the external high-stakes exam, this decision is a little easier to make. I know that if I were back in the public school classroom again, and both my effectiveness as a teacher and the effectiveness of my school were being determined on the basis of my students' performances on an annual state-wide accountability test, you can safely bet that I'd use last-chance formative assessment—with gusto! I'd develop a dress rehearsal exam to parallel any upcoming high-stakes test for which I had instructional responsibilities—or, even better, I'd use one developed collaboratively by my school's teachers or, perhaps, by my district's central office personnel. Using a test developed by others would save me some time, and it would usually reflect a greater pool of expertise.

As for the second type of big test—a teacher-developed one, meant to be the capper on instruction aimed at an especially significant curricular aim—the question is whether the goal is *significant enough* to merit last-chance formative assessment. That's right; the decision rests solely on the teacher's professional judgment. And this professional judgment revolves totally around a teacher's perception regarding the significance of the curricular aim being pursued. Yes, most teachers can—if asked to do so—rank the relative importance of the educational goals they want their students to attain. Those rankings will usually flow from the "future importance" of the skill or body of knowledge embodied in a given curricular aim. Teachers need to grapple with a straightforward question—namely, *"How crucial is it, for a student's in-school success or post-school success, to master the curricular aim now being instructionally pursued?"* This question is easier to frame than it is to answer, but that's what the "How significant?" question boils down to. Teachers need to ask themselves if students, who fail to master the goal will be educationally crippled in some way. If the answer is yes, then an application of last-chance formative assessment is in order.

Choice-Point 2: Whether the Upcoming Assessment Is Adequately Diagnostic

As noted, a dress rehearsal exam must be diagnostic. It must be capable of supplying the teacher with information about where it is, *specifically,* that students most need additional instruction. What this means in practical terms is that there must be a sufficient number of test items for each skill, subskill, or body of knowledge being assessed so that, based on this subset of items, a teacher can draw a reasonably valid inference about every student's mastery status. Moreover, to the extent possible, these items should represent the full range of whatever skill or knowledge is being assessed. So, for example, if a particular skill being promoted in class and measured on a dress rehearsal exam incorporates three subskills, care should be taken to include test items covering all three subskills, not just one. When educators make inferences about students' mastery of a given curricular aim, the items being used to permit a *valid* inference should be sufficient in number and a satisfactory representation of what is being assessed.

Currently, many commercial vendors are selling what are generally referred to as "interim tests," that is, tests intended to be clones of whatever high-stakes tests are in place. Interim tests, usually administered every few months, can often predict with considerable accuracy how well a given student is apt to perform—*overall*—on the upcoming high-stakes test. However, these interim tests, often marketed as "diagnostic," are frequently not diagnostic in any meaningful sense of that term. They do not contain a sufficient number of items measuring each skill or body of knowledge being assessed so that teachers can tell *which skills* or *which bodies of knowledge* their students are having trouble with. So, although interim tests can tell teachers which students are apt to flop on "the real test," those tests usually don't give teachers the information they'd need to prevent that flopping.

The proper use of interim assessments presents a particularly thorny problem for teachers who work in districts where district officials have already developed or purchased off-the-shelf interim tests that claim to be diagnostic but really aren't. In some instances, teachers are urged to review students' performances, *item by item*, in order to figure out what it is that students can or can't do. Just ask any teacher who's tried to make instructional sense from an avalanche of per-item student performances to tell you how useful that mind-numbing exercise has been. Remember, unless there are enough items on an assessment to permit a teacher to come up with a reasonably accurate estimate of a student's mastery of particular skills or bodies of knowledge, proclamations of diagnostic grandeur are flat-out false.

Clearly, if you happen to be a teacher in a setting where a non-diagnostic interim test must be administered periodically, then you'll need to do just that. However, don't fool yourself or your colleagues. The use of such interim assessments is not consonant with the sort of diagnostically dependent last-chance application of formative assessment being described here. Although it seems to make sense to periodically assess students, at this writing there is scant evidence that interim assessment has much payoff for students. Put simply, interim tests may not be worth what they cost *or* the time that administering them takes away from instruction. After a careful review of extant evidence regarding the merits of interim assessments, Arter (2010) drew this conclusion:

> Currently, there is stronger evidence supporting the large impact of classroom-level formative assessment practices than supporting the use of interim assessments, so, if we're going to use scarce resources wisely, we should focus on what the preponderance of evidence indicates is the best use of assessment in the service of student learning. (p. 2)

For the last-chance application of formative assessment to be productive, teachers need evidence from "dress rehearsal" tests that translates readily into a teacher's spotting where students need more instructional support. Absent such diagnostic cues, this application of formative assessment makes no sense.

Choice-Point 3: What the Potential Instructional Adjustment Will Be

Finally, assuming that a suitably diagnostic dress rehearsal exam can be acquired or built, the teacher will need to examine the detailed evidence it generates and decide on a targeted course of instruction to remediate diagnostically identified deficits. So the third choice in this application of formative assessment calls for teachers to consider what needed instruction might stem from using a dress rehearsal exam, then schedule and administer the dress rehearsal exam so there will be adequate instructional time to tackle any assessment-identified deficits in students' mastery.

Yes, as is often the case, successful implementation of the formative assessment process calls for *planning* on the teacher's part. For this last-chance application of formative assessment, a teacher needs to think through in advance—at least in general terms—what sort of instruction might be provided if students display shortcomings with respect to whatever is being measured by a dress rehearsal exam. A teacher can't say for certain where students will be having trouble. After all, that's why the dress-rehearsal exam is being administered in the first place. But what a teacher can do is engage in some "if-then" thinking. For example, suppose a dress rehearsal assessment measured students' mastery of three high-level cognitive skills as well as two different bodies of knowledge. In such a situation, a teacher might simply do a bit of if-then analyzing for each of those five assessed outcomes. What might be done, for instance, if the students stumble on Skill One? What sorts of fix-it instruction might be employed? And how long might it take? How about if students struggle with Skill Two? For all the curricular targets being assessed on the dress rehearsal exam, a teacher should do at least a brief spin-through regarding what might be done if students display weaknesses that warrant instructional attention.

Realistically, many of these general instructional plans are not likely to be needed. But some may be, and teachers who have devoted at least some time to potential instructional particulars, and to their likely duration, will be in a better position to profit from a dress rehearsal exam's results

We can turn now to a fictional teacher who has decided to give this application of formative assessment a try. Again, when you read the interview, try to focus on the decisions the interviewed teacher made and the reasons underlying those decisions.

In the Classroom

Carol Clay has taught 4th graders for almost five years at Public School (P.S.) 204, a center-city elementary school on the eastern seaboard. This is her first teaching job, and she loves it, even though her classes are larger than she would prefer—usually running a few more than 30 students each year. Most of her students are African American and Hispanic, and they come from low-income families in which few parents have had more than a year or two of post-secondary education.

Consistent with a federal accountability law, each year from 3rd grade on, the students in P.S. 204 take a major exam in both reading and mathematics. During the past two years, the students at Carol's school have substantially outperformed students elsewhere in the district—to the degree that the district's school board has taken notice. Several weeks ago, in fact, the board hired five retired teachers for a special assignment. They were called in to help the board determine why P.S. 204 students were doing so well on the state's accountability test in hopes of transferring some of whatever's going on there to other district schools. The retired teachers are to monitor events in Carol's school in the weeks leading up to the annual test administration date and then make a report to the board.

Charlene Hunter, a retired elementary teacher, has been assigned to spend an entire week observing Carol's classes. Per an arrangement with the other teachers on her monitoring team, she will focus on mathematics instruction. At the close of the week, she will sit down with Carol to discuss what she has seen.

Key Classroom Events

On Charlene's first day as an observer, Carol explained what she had in her planning book for the week. She mentioned that her math instruction would be heavily influenced by the results of an almost hour-long "dress rehearsal" exam the students had taken on the previous Friday. This test addressed four prominent math content standards that 4th graders would be expected to demonstrate mastery of on the annual exam: number concepts, basic operations, measurement, and estimation. Charlene asked Carol for a copy of this exam and, reviewing it, saw that it had four sections, each of which centered on one of the four state-specified math content standards for 4th grade. Each section of Carol's dress rehearsal test contained both selected-response questions (usually multiple-choice items) and constructed-response questions (usually short-answer or even one-word-answer items). Carol indicated that she had allowed her students about 50 minutes to take the test, but had split it into two 25-minute sessions on the same day—sessions separated by other instruction as well as by lunch and recess. Carol also gave Charlene a copy of the test's results, and Charlene saw immediately that the students had performed quite wonderfully on two of the state content standards (number concepts and measurement), but had scored rather poorly on the other two standards (basic operations and estimation).

What Charlene observed during the week, then, was Carol's focus on the two areas where her students had not performed well: basic operations and estimation. Approximately three fourths of every day's math instruction was devoted to the basic operations of adding, subtracting, multiplication, and division. The remaining one-fourth of math instruction dealt with how students can make "reasonable, not pinpoint-accurate, estimates." For both main topics, Carol provided clear explanations of how those math operations worked, followed by guided and independent practice. Each day, students completed and turned in a set of exercises that, Charlene saw, were very similar to the kinds of items that appeared on Carol's dress rehearsal exam. These exercises were always returned to students on the following day; they were marked but ungraded, and accompanied by written suggestions about students' weaknesses and what might be done to address those weaknesses.

As the week progressed, Charlene saw substantial improvement, almost across the board, in students' abilities to carry out basic mathematical operations, although a number of students continued to have difficulty dividing without a calculator. Similarly, students' prowess in making "reasonable" estimates appeared to improve discernibly during the week. On Friday, Carol used a total-class assessment activity in which students responded to orally presented questions on individual erasable whiteboards. As far as Charlene could tell, students seemed to do well on these whiteboard assessments.

At the end of the week, Charlene held what she described as her "debriefing" interview with Carol.

The Interview of Carol Clay

by School-Board Envoy Charlene Hunter

First off, Carol, I want to tell you how much I appreciated your willingness to let me sit in on your class—and for a whole week! You have been very gracious to me, and I thank you. As you know, the district board asked me and four other retired teachers to help them understand why your school has done so well on the state's annual exams. I'm hoping my report will clarify what you and your colleagues have been so successful in doing here at P.S. 204. Although I was observing everything that went on in your class, I was asked by the members of our team to concentrate on mathematics, so that's what I hope we can focus on during this interview.

I have to say, you were really as unobtrusive an observer as I've ever had in my classes! After that first day, Monday, I don't think the kids even knew you were here. So math is what you're most interested in, Charlene? OK, what can I tell you about my math instruction?

Well, for openers, I'd like to learn more about the test that you referred to as your "dress rehearsal exam." I appreciated your letting me examine a copy and showing me your students' results. Is this kind of practice testing some sort of schoolwide initiative?

That's a good question, and it's the key to why our school does so well on the state exams. The entire staff, starting with the principal and assistant principal, is committed to the frequent use of the formative assessment process. Are you familiar with this approach? The essence of it is that teachers use students' performance data to determine if instructional adjustments are necessary. Almost all of us here use formative assessment in one way or another.

Anyway, what you saw in my class this week is what's called the "last-chance instructional adjustment" application of the formative assessment process. It calls for teachers, whenever an important exam is approaching—and the state accountability tests certainly fit this definition—to assess their students' mastery of whatever will be on that exam. Teachers then provide a sort of last-minute dose of instruction for anything students appear to be weak in. We refer to these tests as "dress rehearsal exams," because they are, almost literally, a dress rehearsal for our students' subsequent performances on the state accountability tests.

I started hearing talk of formative assessment in the year before I retired, but I never used it myself. Is this last-chance approach the only way the teachers at P.S. 204 use formative assessment?

No, definitely not. We use it in all kinds of ways—most often, I think, to gather in-class performance data and make basically instant adjustments to what we are doing. For instance, we might explain content a different way, or provide more or different practice activities. We also use it a lot to adjust our units. We look at our students' scores on quizzes, their homework performances, and so on, and use this data to customize instruction so we can address areas of identified need. I think that most of us use this last-chance application just one time a year, during the weeks leading up to the state tests, although a handful of teachers do use it during the year in connection with their own more important tests. That's not something I do at this point, but one day I might give it a try.

How do you and your colleagues make sure that your dress rehearsal exams are diagnostic? I assume that if those tests don't give you data specific enough to inform your subsequent instructional decisions, they're not of much use.

You're right. They have to be carefully constructed. In math, for example, the other 4th grade teachers and I put a lot of effort into making sure that there are enough items measuring each of the four math content standards. That way, when we score our students' exams, we get a clear picture of exactly where student's shortcomings are so that we can focus our last-minute instruction accordingly. We try to include at least eight items per content standard.

I noticed that you seemed to devote a week's worth of instruction to the two content standards that your students struggled with most. Yet I believe there's still another week before your students will be taking the state tests. Don't you want to schedule this last-minute instruction to take place at the last minute? Why the extra week?

You noticed that, huh? I'm glad. One thing about using this application of formative assessment is that you have figure out how to fit the dress rehearsal exam and subsequent test-informed, last-minute instruction into your schedule. So I have to look at the date of the accountability test and decide when it makes the most sense for me to administer the dress rehearsal, knowing that I need to allot enough time to address the weaknesses that the dress rehearsal results will uncover before the state testing day arrives. This year, I figured wrong. I assumed—based on last year's class—that my students would need additional instruction related to all four of the math content standards being assessed, but as it turned out, they didn't. They did really, really well on two of the content standards, so that instead of needing two weeks for adjusted, additional instruction, I only needed one week to refocus on basic operations and estimation.

So what will you do during your math classes next week? Even more instruction related to basic operations and estimation?

Well, you may have noticed that right at the close of today's math session I asked my kids a series of questions dealing with those two topics. Those were the questions they answered on their whiteboards, and, as you also may have noticed, most of the students did really well. So, no, I don't plan to reteach next week what I did this past week. My students now seem to be ready to tackle all four content standards that the math accountability tests will assess, so I may only do a "once-over-lightly" review of all the math content one day next week. Actually, I may steal some of the regularly allotted math time to focus on content that will be included on the reading portion of the state tests. I'll be giving a dress rehearsal exam for the reading standards on Monday.

I appreciate your frankness, Carol. What you are telling me is that formative assessment, at least this last-chance version of it, also calls on teachers to make pedagogical choices. And because teachers are human, those choices won't always be 100 percent perfect.

Right. I've made mistakes, and I'm sure to make them again. Actually, though, what my colleagues and I have read about formative assessment is really comforting on that point. The research shows that formative assessment is such a powerful way of improving instruction that teachers don't have to obsess over "doing it perfectly." You can do it lots of ways, and students still benefit. So, yes, I wish I'd timed my last-minute instruction to actually be more last-minute, but the assessment data I've gathered tells me I can be confident my students will do well on the state's math test.

An Interview Look-Back

Although Carol uses this particular variant of formative assessment as a way of getting her students to sparkle on the annual state accountability tests, it seems that she does not think it suitable to use in connection with her own important, unit-ending, summative teacher-made tests. This choice aptly illustrates that while there are several different applications of formative assessment, a teacher should always decide which, if any, of those approaches is most compatible with the students, the curricular aims involved, and his or her own distinctive personality and pedagogical style.

In the interview, Carol also revealed that she and her colleagues make sure to include a sufficiently large subset of items measuring each of the content standards being assessed. Some teachers would probably try to get by with fewer items per curricular aim, but it seems she prefers to err in the direction of too many items than too few items—an appropriate choice, I think, given the dress rehearsal exam's diagnostic purpose.

Regarding whether there was sufficient time for students' diagnosed problems to be addressed instructionally, in this instance we saw that Carol had misestimated by allowing more time than students' actual test data indicated was needed. This "mistake" by the teacher illustrates a more general point: There is no "must-do" playbook that good formative assessors will follow and bad formative assessors will violate. When using formative assessment properly, all that teachers try to do is use assessments to supply evidence about how well instruction is going so that, if it isn't going well enough, instructional adjustments can save the day. Will teachers always make the right moves when implementing formative assessment? Unfortunately, they will not. But if a teacher such as Carol makes a conscientious effort to arrive at the best decisions regarding how and when to assess students so needed instructional adjustments can be made, based on the resulting evidence, then the teacher's students are almost certain to learn better than students who are not on the receiving end of formative assessment.

Reflection Questions

1. If you were advising a group of beginning teachers on when it made sense to carry out last-chance formative assessment in advance of an end-of-unit exam, what sorts of factors would you suggest they consider?

2. Do you work in a school where the use of interim exams (also referred to as "benchmark" or "periodic" assessments) is policy? If so, do they meet the standards of "suitability for formative assessment" outlined in this chapter?

3. Do you believe a teacher could be an effective user of formative assessment without utilizing this last-chance application of the formative assessment process? Why or why not?

4. How might you employ this application of formative assessment in your own classroom? Consider all the choice-points discussed in this chapter.

7

Students'
Learning Tactic
Adjustments

So far, we've considered three different applications of formative assessment, all of which revolve around teachers' adjustments to current or upcoming instructional activities. In this chapter, we're going to be looking at a very different application of the formative assessment process—one focused not on adjustments by *teachers* but rather on adjustments by *students*. More specifically, the chapter addresses how students can use formative assessment to alter their own learning tactics.

A *learning tactic*, as noted back in Chapter 1, is simply the way a student is attempting to learn something. To illustrate, some students like to study alone, while some prefer to study with others. Certain students tackle complex assignments by trying to break what's complex into separate parts that can be studied one part at a time; other students prefer to tackle complex material all in one complicated bundle. Truly, if we were to list the possible permutations of students' approaches to learning, such a list would be long indeed. Still, depending on the particular students involved—and the specifics of what they are currently studying—some learning tactics definitely work better than others. If whatever a student is doing to learn something isn't working—as revealed by assessment results—then the obvious solution for the student is to do something else. And that's the point of the fourth application of formative assessment, described in *TA1* as Level 2 formative assessment: students reviewing assessment-elicited evidence for the purpose of making *learning tactic adjustments*.

Implementation Considerations

When I was growing up, a common saying was, "You can lead a horse to water, but you can't make it drink." I never verified the accuracy of this contention because I never owned a horse and had no idea about how one might entice a horse to consume any form of liquid—be it water, lemonade, or hot cocoa. But I did recognize the purpose of this equine axiom: to remind us there are instances when, despite our best efforts to persuade an individual to do something, the actual "doing" depends on the individual's *willingness* to do it.

This particular application of formative assessment includes several nuts-and-bolts choices a teacher must make—such as choosing the sorts of assessments to use. But what really distinguishes this application is that, although the teacher can create a set of circumstances so that it is in a student's best interest to adjust any learning tactics in need of adjusting, *it is up to the student* to decide whether or not to do so.

The realization that formative assessment aimed at learning tactic adjustments is essentially out of a teacher's hands can disincline some teachers from even wanting to try it out. Why go to all the trouble of supplying students with assessment results if it's possible students *won't* choose to shape up their learning tactics? Well, it's because the potential educational payoffs are worth it. Let's see why.

Autonomous, Self-Correcting Learners

Optimally, schools should be graduating young men and women who can select their own goals, chart their own courses of action to attain those goals, and then employ whatever ability and effort they can muster to achieve their aspirations. It makes sense, then, to prepare students to be truly autonomous learners, not dependent on their teachers or on anyone else to tell them what to study and how to study it.

This is the moment when the fourth application of formative assessment rumbles to the rescue. It's about showing students how to become *self-correcting learners*—that is, learners who continually monitor the merits of their chosen goal-attainment tactics by assessing the consequences of those tactics. While students' in-school behaviors are not perfectly predictive of those students' future behaviors, teachers can be reasonably confident that most autonomous, self-correcting learners will become autonomous, self-correcting adults. Is this not an educational goal worthy of pursuit?

The promotion of learning tactic adjustments helps create students who know where they are headed instructionally and who, based on assessment evidence, *routinely* evaluate how successful their efforts have been in getting them there. The point of this fourth application of formative assessment is to help students not only arrive at a better way to learn specific things in school, but also think about everything they do in life—and how they might do it more successfully.

Affect Trumps Cognition

Getting students to monitor and adjust their own learning tactics calls for teachers to delve into the affective domain. Simply put, the success of this application of formative assessment depends on a student's *disposition*—specifically, students' willingness to monitor the effectiveness of their own learning tactics and make adjustments when it seems necessary. For this reason, I firmly believe that teachers who wish to adapt this application of formative assessment need to devote less effort to letting students see how the application works and more effort to getting students to *want to use it*.

There's ample written guidance on how to promote cognitive curricular outcomes—an ever-increasing collection of research-supported instructional techniques teachers might incorporate into their practice. In contrast, many teachers know almost nothing about techniques for modifying students' affect. Accordingly, I'd like to present brief sketches of the three most potent procedures for altering students' affect, namely, *modeling, reinforcement,* and *contiguity* techniques.

Modeling. This technique relies on an esteemed individual (often the teacher) displaying behaviors reflective of whatever affect the teacher hopes students will adopt. To illustrate, if a social studies teacher wants students to acquire an ongoing interest in daily news events, she could refer regularly to current news developments, mentioning that the information had been published in the daily newspaper or on the Internet.

The most effective models for inspiring a change in students' affect are always individuals whom students really admire. So, for example, a teacher might enlist the help of several former students who, during a class visit, recount the positive *personal* payoffs of taking a more assertive role in monitoring the success of their own learning tactics. To the extent that those former students are well known and popular, at least some of the teacher's current students may be inclined to adopt similar attitudes toward this kind of student-governed formative assessment.

Reinforcement. A second technique for influencing students' affect involves the teacher's reinforcing even the most modest of student behaviors consonant with this fourth application of formative assessment. Maybe the teacher compliments Billy after class on the day that Billy carefully reviews the feedback written on his returned essay rather than just folding it up and sticking it into his textbook. Or perhaps the teacher sends home a brief note of commendation after James confides that he thinks he'll do better on the next unit if he gives solo studying a try instead of continuing to work in a study group with his often-disruptive friends.

Contiguity. A third way to influence students' affect involves the use of contiguity, which is the encouraging of desirable behaviors through positive association. It's easy to confuse contiguity with reinforcement, as both rely on a teacher's use of positive actions, conditions, or rewards. In reinforcement, the teacher supplies a positive stimulus—such as an expression of approval—only *after* students have displayed the sought-for behavior. With contiguity, the teacher works to establish a positive stimulus whenever students have an opportunity to engage in the sought-for behavior—even if students have never actually behaved in the way a teacher hopes they will. To illustrate, the teacher might go to great lengths to make the return of assessment results—results that students will be asked to review and use as the basis for potential learning tactic adjustments—into a pleasant occasion. This might involve praising the apparent seriousness with which students completed the assessment, for example, and celebrating the illuminating payoffs of each incorrect answer. The idea is to squash negativity so that positives prevail.

What I've provided here are just capsule treatments of three remarkably complex procedures. I encourage teachers who are serious about fostering affective change to dig into the viscera of these concepts far more deeply and perhaps investigate works by Erwin (2010) and Sullo (2009).

Does every teacher who attempts to promote students' learning tactic adjustments have to become conversant with a repertoire of affect-altering techniques? No, but they do need to understand that this application of formative assessment will fizzle if students do not personally *choose* to adopt it, and, because the concepts here are likely to be new to them, it's up to the teacher to make the case for adoption.

This Application's Key Choice-Points

Teachers using formative assessment focused on students' learning tactic adjustments will face decisions about the kinds of assessments to use and when to collect the assessment evidence. However, because those choices have been dealt with sufficiently in earlier chapters, we can concentrate here on the three new decisions (see Figure 7.1) that are particularly pertinent to this application.

FIGURE 7.1

Three Choice-Points for Facilitating Students' Use of Formative Assessment to Adjust Learning Tactics

1. **How to clarify students' understanding of curricular aims.** In what ways can a teacher best ensure that students understand what is being sought from them?

2. **What the procedural particulars will be.** How should this application of formative assessment actually operate? When will assessment evidence be collected? How will the results be communicated to students? How will students' adjustment decisions be guided or supported?

3. **How to nurture the appropriate affect.** What general strategy or techniques will be effective in getting this particular set of students to willingly embrace this formative assessment application?

Choice-Point 1: How to Clarify Students' Understanding of Curricular Aims

It is difficult, if not impossible, to think of any instructional scenario in which students wouldn't benefit from an enhanced understanding of what they're expected to achieve. In this particular application of formative assessment, students' grasp of curricular expectations is especially critical. How can students possibly evaluate how well current learning tactics are helping them master a set of curricular aims if they don't know what those aims actually are?

For purposes of illustration, let's assume that a teacher is preparing a six-week-long instructional unit containing three mandatory curricular aims drawn from official state-defined content standards. There are several sound ways to go about communicating to students the outcomes they are supposed to achieve.

Supply students with the curricular aims. This seems obvious, but it's very powerful and often overlooked. A teacher can simply provide students with an oral and written description of the curricular aims, translated, as necessary, into student-friendly language. The teacher might even open the aims up for class discussion and respond to questions about the meanings of or rationales for particular curricular aims.

Describe the set of evaluative criteria. Curricular aims without evaluative criteria are often empty rhetoric, and a second way to help students grasp what they're supposed to learn is for the teacher to explain what factors will be used to distinguish between wonderful and woeful performances. For example, if an English teacher intends to give considerable weight to written mechanics when judging students' compositions, then it is only fair to let students in on this evaluative intention. One of the best ways to do this is to distribute the rubrics that will be used to evaluate students' responses. Rubrics, replete with evaluative criteria and the weights applied to these criteria, can be used in any subject when an assignment incorporates constructed-response tasks. With a reasonable handle on how responses are going to be evaluated, students can do a better job judging their progress toward mastering the curricular aims set.

Supply examples of good and bad performance. Finally, teachers can enhance students' understanding of curricular aims by sharing divergent exemplars of previous students' performances: responses judged both excellent and inadequate, based on the announced evaluative criteria. During the early phases of an instructional unit, when students may be very new to the material, it's a good idea to make these examples quite clear-cut and representative of both *really* excellent and *really* wretched responses. As students' familiarity with the material increases, more nuanced examples of strong and weak responses can be used as illustrations.

To review, a teacher might help students understand what's expected of them through (1) distribution of the curricular aims, restated in student-friendly language; (2) presentation of scoring rubrics containing evaluative criteria that will be used to determine the quality of a student's performance; and (3) provision of strong and weak exemplar responses from previous students. The challenge for a teacher at this initial choice-point is to determine what configuration of activities and materials would most effectively help the particular students in the class understand the nature of the specific curricular outcomes they are supposed to master. In this application of formative assessment, students' understanding of the curricular aims being sought is *an absolute must.*

Choice-Point 2: What the Procedural Particulars Will Be

Many variations of this formative assessment application's procedural particulars are possible, but teachers who use it effectively find they must make decisions about (1) when assessment evidence will be collected, (2) how to quickly and efficiently communicate assessment results to students, (3) how to help students decide whether their assessment performances warrant adjustments in learning tactics, and (4) how to lay out potential learning tactic adjustments for those students who need them. Because this application of formative assessment centers on *students'* actions, once a teacher has made a decision about each of these operations, the teacher must communicate the procedural particulars to students so they'll understand all phases of the process. And, of course, if the ensuing classroom experiences indicate that some features of this procedure need to be altered, the teacher should certainly make those changes, filling students in on the new plans.

Let's briefly consider each of the four key procedural decisions a teacher must make.

When assessment evidence will be collected for consideration. The teacher needs to let students know when to expect the assessments that will generate data for their consideration. Because assessment evidence should be collected near the conclusion of instruction associated with any building blocks in the learning progression being used, students can certainly be informed about these anticipated assessments. Remember, this fourth application of formative assessment hopes to engender a degree of autonomy in students. Autonomous learners have the right to know when assessment—building block or otherwise—is likely to take place. As you'll see in the next chapter, it is possible for a single set of data to be used by both students and the teacher.

How to communicate assessment results to students. Again, teachers who adopt this formative assessment application need to decide how to get results of all assessments back to students as quickly as is practical and in a format that will be most useful to them.

It's important to note that when this application of formative assessment is being used, students' test performances *are almost never graded.* Teachers must stress that tests and quizzes are tools for discovery, not judgment, and that, especially in the early stages of learning, making mistakes is not a bad thing, but a helpful one. Mistakes show both the teacher and the student what needs to be fixed. Of course, in practical terms, this philosophy means that teachers need to review students' performances for the purpose of supplying descriptive feedback on areas of strength and, particularly, on areas of inadequacy. Ideally, teachers will also offer suggestions about potential ways students might deal with those inadequacies. This sort of tailored, constructive feedback takes time for teachers to dispense.

It falls to each teacher to decide how best to transmit assessment results and feedback, based on what that teacher believes will be most instructionally helpful in light of the particular students involved, the curricular aims being pursued, and the time and energy available. Whatever decision the teacher reaches on this issue, the students must be informed of it.

How to help students make the adjust-or-not-adjust decision. This application of formative assessment centers on what students decide to do, not what teachers would like those students to do. But teachers can certainly provide guidance regarding what level of performance might indicate that a learning tactic adjustment is necessary, especially if the class is new to this sort of student adjustment. (These suggestions are akin to the adjustment triggers we dealt with in teacher-adjustment applications of formative assessment.) For example, after distributing assessment results, a teacher might walk the class through a set of simulated results prepared for a fictitious student, explaining how this nonexistent student might arrive at a decision about whether to make a learning tactic adjustment. Depending on the particular classroom environment, the teacher might call for volunteers willing to be the focus of a class discussion about whether the student's learning tactics need to be tinkered with, totally overhauled, or left as is. Or a teacher, having analyzed a set of assessment results, might announce that scores below certain levels—overall or in specific areas—definitely warrant the *consideration* of an adjustment.

As time goes by, students will need less teacher support when it comes to adjustment decisions. However, teachers must always remember that although they can offer advice regarding whether or not their students need to make adjustments in learning tactics, it's up to the student to heed that advice or ignore it entirely. If the teacher has made a reasonable effort to get students to consider adjusting, and those students choose not to do so, then that's regrettably the way this classroom cookie crumbles. Remember, too, that a teacher has other instructional intervention options for addressing learning deficits, and none of these are precluded by the use of this kind of formative assessment. But one thing a teacher can't do is make a student *self-evaluate* unless the student chooses to do so.

How to lay out a menu of potential learning tactic adjustments. Particularly during the early days of this application's installation, teachers will need to spend some meaningful time with the whole class describing what a learning tactic is and, when students have a particular set of assessment evidence before them, laying out a number of possible learning tactic adjustments that might prove successful. This can be very illuminating for students who may believe that the only viable way to learn better is to "study harder."

These adjustment options vary with content, grade levels, and the pedagogical savvy of the teacher. Some that I've seen include "study buddy" programs, in which students sign up to work in pairs on specific skills or bodies of knowledge that cause them trouble, and a peer-tutoring model, in which students who are particularly proficient in a certain areas agree to assist their classmates who are having trouble with those areas. For certain content areas and particular curricular aims, the use of graphic organizers can be illuminating to some students. Other students can profit immensely if they learn how to succinctly summarize what they have read or learned about in other ways. Teachers can, of course, often pick up great ideas about learning tactic adjustments from other teachers.

Choice-Point 3: How to Nurture the Appropriate Affect

If this application of formative assessment does not cause substantially greater numbers of students to become self-evaluators and self-adjustors of their own learning progress, then the application is a waste of students' and teachers' time. So, from the earliest moments of thinking about trying this application, a teacher should think carefully about how to get students on board. The question a teacher must ask is, *"What affect-influencing techniques can I use to get students interested in and excited about using assessment evidence to monitor the success of their learning tactics?"*

In truth, a concerted effort by like-minded colleagues can make a big difference, so the question might be phrased in the plural. And it ought to lead to many collegial discussions. Earlier in the chapter, we looked at three potentially effective ways that teachers can modify students' affect: *modeling, reinforcement,* and *contiguity.* In the abstract, those might sound like interesting notions, but nobody who teaches children can be successful by working solely in the abstract. When experienced teachers discuss this topic, the concepts of modeling, reinforcement, and contiguity may never even come up. What's more likely to emerge are practical, time-tested ideas.

Because of the centrality of students' affective dispositions in this application of formative assessment, teachers interested in using it should become conversant with the rudiments of how to employ self-report inventories for the measurement of students' affect. In *TA1* (Popham, 2008, pp. 104–108), I described how to build anonymously completed self-report inventories suitable for arriving at inferences regarding the affective status of student *groups* (not of individual students—the distinction is key). The creation of such affective inventories is relatively simple and can yield remarkably useful insights regarding how well an instructional strategy is "taking."

OK, now that we've looked at the most important choices to be made when a teacher sets out to tackle this instructional approach that's patently dependent on students' use of classroom assessment evidence, it's time to see what a teacher might be thinking during its implementation. Let's look at a fictional teacher who is currently using an application of formative assessment centered on students' learning tactic adjustments.

In the Classroom

George Lee teaches English at Jordan Creek Middle School, the only middle school in a mid-sized rural community in a southeastern state. He teaches mostly 7th and 8th grade classes, and has been doing so for almost a dozen years. His students are genuinely diverse with respect to both socioeconomic status and ethnicity, and their parents are very involved in the classroom community. George is really happy to be teaching where he's teaching.

Over the past four years, George and six of his colleagues at Jordan Creek have been using a version of formative assessment that places a heavy emphasis on students' self-monitoring of their learning and making any necessary adjustments in their learning tactics. (Five of the six teachers also routinely use other variations of formative assessment to adjust their own instructional activities.) It is generally conceded that George is the most knowledgeable of the school's teachers who are using this kind of formative assessment. During the monthly meeting, when these teachers get together to share practices and lessons learned, he is almost always the one who has done the most between-meeting thinking and reading about formative assessment.

At a recent school board meeting, several parents raised the issue of why the district's two elementary schools were not attempting to follow in the middle school's footsteps and "help students become self-correcting learners." So Gail Miller, a long-term board member who had been an elementary teacher in the district for almost 20 years, volunteered pay a visit to Jordan Creek Middle School to get a better understanding of the middle school's highly praised efforts to foster independent learning. She called the school's principal, who then arranged for her to observe of one of George's 8th grade English classes.

Key Classroom Events

The class that Gail sat in on was in the midst of a five-week unit dealing with punctuation rules. Thirty-four 8th graders were present in George's classroom, which was furnished with both movable student desks and three large tables suitable for group work. As Gail quickly discerned, George's current lesson focused on the proper use of commas. Taped to the whiteboard at the front of the classroom were five pieces of paper, each bearing a numbered rule for comma usage.

As the class session opened up, George passed back exams that students had taken the day before. An 8th grader sitting near Gail volunteered to show her his exam paper, and she noted that it had no grade—just written notes indicating which of the five comma-usage rules the student had had trouble applying correctly: "Number 2: Setting off introductory elements" and "Number 3: Separating elements in a series."

After giving students a few minutes to review the feedback on their corrected papers, George said, "OK, now, go ahead and determine the percent of mistakes you have made on each of the five comma-usage rules, then decide if you need to make an adjustment in how you're trying to learn each. In a few minutes, we're going to break into Review Stations, where you can talk over particular rules and where they apply. If you decide you do not need to adjust your learning tactics, you may do one of the following: Read your assigned novella; work on your expository essay—remember, this is due in two weeks; or come and speak to me about any aspect of punctuation or composition."

Then, as Gail watched, George called out the names of five students and gave each a number. These students removed the individual comma-rule statements posted on the whiteboard, taped them to their desks, and dragged their desks to various spots in the room. They were setting up the so-called "Review Stations." At the teacher's signal, students got up and moved to the labeled station of their choice, where the student leaders conducted a short analysis of the station's comma rule and its applicability. Students shared their exam papers, looked through notebooks of examples, and asked and answered one another's questions. Every 10 minutes, George called for a shift. Gail noted that while most students moved freely from station to station, some stayed at the same station for longer review. A few stayed at the same station for three sessions in a row.

Gail observed with interest, as students really seemed to be working on their own. Although there was a buzz of small-group conversation, the noise level suggested active learning, not distracted students. As the period continued, she saw various students return to their desks and pull out their novellas or open their notebooks and apparently get to work on the essay activity. Several students waited their turn to speak individually with George.

Although most of George's students were doing what he wanted them to do, Gail noticed about four girls and two boys who did not take part in any Review Station activity, but also did not seem to be working particularly hard either on any of the other activity options. George spoke briefly to each of these students, but he didn't seem displeased with their behavior or with their apparent unwillingness to become engaged.

As the period drew to a close, George assigned a new set of homework exercises covering the use of colons and semicolons. He also thanked the entire class for "staying on task in getting a better handle on the five comma-usage rules." As the students filed out of George's classroom, Gail concluded that she had rarely seen a class session in which the teacher engaged in so little of what most people usually call "teaching." She looked forward to asking George many questions.

The Interview of George Lee

by School Board Member Gail Miller

Thanks so much, George, for letting me watch your class. I found it really interesting. As I mentioned, I used to be an elementary school teacher in the district, and I'm really intrigued by the things you and the other teachers at Jordan Creek are up to with respect to formative assessment. Those two articles you sent me by e-mail were very helpful. As I understand it, what I just watched was a particular use of formative assessment focused on students adjusting how they are trying to learn things. When I've heard of formative assessment from other educators, it seemed their focus was on teachers adjusting their instruction. Are both of these things formative assessment?

Yes, Gail, they are. Formative assessment is something teachers can use to adjust their own instruction, and it's also something students can use to adjust their learning tactics. I've personally been using it in both ways for about three years now.

Well, as I mentioned to your principal on the phone, at the last board meeting, a delegation of parents came to us talking about your school's emphasis on getting more students to be self-directed, self-correcting learners. They were worried that their elementary-age children were missing out on something really special. So I'm here on behalf of the board to learn more about the process so we will know how to respond to those parental inquiries.

As I'm sure you saw during this class, my 8th graders are getting quite good at monitoring their own progress and adjusting how they are trying to learn something if the evidence says they're falling short. That's how I present it to them. What they're doing is keeping track of their actions . . . evaluating their learning inputs based on my assessment of the learning outputs, and then changing the input if they decide they want a different, better output. Now, as a teacher yourself, you know that commas are very difficult for some students. So I'm really pleased that so many of them, once they had a chance to look at their own performances on yesterday's exam, decided to get some additional, different instruction dealing with the five comma-usage rules.

How can you tell if this approach is working, George? I know when I used to teach, every few years we had a new and different "latest instructional breakthrough" that our district administrators told us we were supposed to install. Is this version of formative assessment one of those "next nifty thing" fads?

You know, no, the research suggests it isn't. There's a considerable amount of empirical research evidence indicating that both the "teacher adjustments" and the "student adjustments" applications of formative assessments work, and work well. What's particularly interesting to me is that the research studies indicate there is not one "anointed" way to make formative assessment work. The five other teachers here at our school who use this particular application of formative assessment—the one focused on students' learning tactics—all seem to use it in slightly different ways. What we all do, though, is give students assessment evidence regarding their performances and then encourage the students to make learning tactic adjustments if they wish to do so.

So their wishes are a big factor here. Attitude and motivation must be a big part of making this work.

Without a doubt. If we can't get our students to tackle their own learning, then this version of formative assessment surely won't work—nor will it do any good for those students once they leave school. You see, Gail, and I hope you can make this point to the other board members, what we are trying to do here is create *inde-pendent* learners, and by that, I mean kids who not only can monitor how well their approaches to learning are working, but who know what sorts of evidence to rely on as they do that monitoring.

Students who routinely evaluate the effectiveness of their efforts by drawing on relevant evidence while in school will tend to be adults who evaluate the merits of their efforts with relevant evidence. And isn't that what we want for our children?

I noticed that, at a certain point in the lesson, you set up several options for your students: the Review Stations, the assigned novella, the expository essay they were to complete in two weeks, or a conference with you. Where did you come up with those alternatives? I'm assuming that you were hoping most students would gravitate to the Review Stations, where the focus was on the comma usage rules . . . .

Yes, that's right. What you saw today, Gail, was a fairly common model teachers use when they decide to let students make their own instruction-monitoring decisions. I try to set up most class sessions so there are clear study options depending on whether students' assessment evidence inclines them to seek more or, equally often, different instruction.

Did you notice the students who had a one-on-one conference with me instead of going to a Review Station? Those particular kids have found that when they're running into trouble or getting confused, talking directly with me works out better for them than small-group work does. All three of these students have also opted into a formal "parent on call" program at home. Their moms or dads have agreed to provide a specified amount of homework-assistance time—15 to 30 minutes—every night.

But do you always have Review Stations? The five stations and the five comma-usage rules worked out very well, but what about other content and educational objectives?

The key is to try your best to set up alternative ways that students might learn things. And, as you say, sometimes small-group work based on peer teaching, which is what you saw today, just isn't feasible or appropriate. So sometimes I set up two groups, one led by

me and one led by a pair of students who seem particularly knowledgeable about the subject matter or particularly adept at the skill
we're focusing on. And when all else fails, there's always the good
old "read silently at your desk" option. My colleagues here at Jordan
Creek, the ones who are using formative assessment frequently—
especially this application of it—get together on a monthly basis to
brainstorm and discuss different effective ways that kids can learn.
It's not always easy to come up with realistic options, but when we
can, and when students realize that it's their choice about how they
study something, the payoffs are tremendously positive.

*OK, to backtrack a minute, what about the students who aren't will-
ing to make that choice—aren't willing to tackle their own learning? I
mean, I saw students who either weren't participating or really didn't
seem to be "into" what you were doing. You spoke to those students,
but you didn't seem particularly bothered by their lack of involvement. What about students like these?*

You're right. Student attitude and motivation are essential in this
kind of formative assessment, and so far, I have been unable to get
those particular youngsters to buy into this approach. I've actually
held conferences with each of those students and their parents, trying to persuade all involved that this student-in-control model can
work. Oh, I still try to teach them the same way that I would have
if I were not using formative assessment, but I think this was one
of the really tough realizations I had to accept when using a version of formative assessment that ultimately depends on whether
students will voluntarily do what you hope they will do. This is the
third year I have been using this approach, and each year I have
been unsuccessful with about a half-dozen of my students. I've had
some lengthy conversations with the other teachers who use this
approach, and not one of them reports being able to get 100 percent
of their students to fully embrace the process. But we stick with it
because we believe that if we can incline *most* of our students to

become autonomous learners—without educationally penalizing the students who don't—then we should continue.

But you don't let your annual crop of a half-dozen "nonbelievers" languish, do you? What becomes of them?

Oh, of course not. But because they aren't interested in making their own adjustments in learning tactics, I get to make those decisions all by myself! I focus on giving these kids plenty of more-traditional instruction and intervene with support when the evidence suggests it's necessary.

What would you like the board to know about this approach to teaching, George? Do you think that those parents were right? That we should be encouraging our district's elementary teachers to be using formative assessment aimed at students' learning tactic adjustments?

I would love to see all our elementary teachers trying this. It would certainly be a great thing for those of us using it here at Jordan Creek, because it would mean more of our incoming students would arrive ready to get to work using it with us.

When you talk to the board, I hope you will describe the central idea about this kind of formative assessment and why we value it so much. I think you have a solid grasp of its essentials. But, Gail, if the board does decide to promote the use of this process among elementary teachers—and even high school teachers—please realize that you will need to supply them with professional development support and adequate time to work out the kinks in what they are doing. This isn't an easy way to teach. But it is a good way to teach.

An Interview Look-Back

It is impossible to understand everything going on in a classroom based on a one-period observation. During the interview, Gail tries to get at three important issues: (1) the purpose of this application of formative assessment, (2) how to structure instructional activities to permit "learner's choice," and (3) the issue of whether it will work for all students.

In response, George stressed that the payoff for those students who adopted this formative assessment variant, with its emphasis on evaluating actions according to the outcomes of those actions, could be enormous, down the road in their school careers and for the rest of their lives. Starting students down this sort of evaluative highway will surely benefit many of them. George also stressed the significance of the affective component in this approach to formative assessment. If students do not *want* to use this way of monitoring their own work, then they most assuredly will not use it. Teachers who use this application must work to solve that affective puzzle.

George also tried to spell out how to set up class activities so that several effective learning-tactic adjustment options are available to students. Clearly, teachers who implement this version of formative assessment are making a serious commitment to differentiated instruction, laying out the instructional variants but also leaving students to self-select which variant is right for them.

Finally, George described honestly what teachers who use this approach must be willing to expect. It may not work with every child. Getting 100 percent adoption and 100 percent payoff for students should always be a teacher's goal, but don't despair if not all students hop happily aboard the Autonomous Learner Bandwagon. Simply try to make it work for as many students as possible.

Reflection Questions

1. If you were advising a school principal on how to make a case for adopting this kind of formative assessment on a schoolwide basis, what would you recommend? What do you think it would take to convince a teacher to try this dramatic change from "instruction as usual"?

2. Of the three techniques described for altering students' affective dispositions—*modeling, reinforcement,* and *contiguity*—which do you think most teachers would find the easiest to use when trying to get students to embrace this kind of formative assessment? Which would be the most difficult? Which do you think would be most effective for the students *you* teach?

3. Why is clarifying curricular aims for students particularly critical for this application of formative assessment?

4. If you were a teacher whose students had no prior experience in monitoring their own learning successes, and you wanted to implement this chapter's application of formative assessment, how long do you think it would take before most of your students had attained a reasonable level of confidence in using this approach? On what do you base that estimate?

5. Think about a unit of instruction that you teach and how you might restructure it to incorporate this application of formative assessment. Consider all the choice-points discussed in this chapter.

8

Classroom Climate Shifts

"Putting it all together" is an expression often used by sports teams, musical groups, and business organizations. It signifies a moment when the individuals involved in an enterprise have been able to synergize their separate efforts in such a way that the results are spectacularly successful. If you're a member of a group that has "put it all together," you surely found it to be genuinely gratifying. You knew you had a hand in achieving something rarely achieved, something truly wonderful. Well, the fifth and final application of formative assessment represents a putting-it-all-together possibility for every teacher. To be a teacher who successfully pulls off this chapter's formative assessment application is to be a teacher who has accomplished something quite special.

In previous chapters of this book, we have looked at four applications of the formative assessment process, three focused on teachers' adjustment decisions and one focused on students' adjustment decisions. Although each of the four applications is discernibly different from the others, all four of them are aimed at the same outcome—improved student learning.

Well, what would happen if we were to coalesce all four of those different applications into a single, harmonized set of instructional activities? What would happen, in other words, if a teacher were to use all four of the previously considered applications at one time?

The answer is that the teacher will have created a brand new application of formative assessment—a blending of the four that lays the foundation for a *classroom climate shift.*

As mentioned way back in the Introduction, in *TA1,* I identified several "levels" of formative assessment, the third of which was focused on bringing about a classroom climate shift. What was referred to in that earlier book as Level 3 formative assessment is being identified in this book as the fifth application of the formative assessment process. There is no difference between the two.

A Closer Look at Classroom Climate

What is classroom climate, and why should teachers even consider fussing with it? This two-part question needs to be answered satisfactorily if a teacher ever intends to be successful when implementing formative assessment aimed at a classroom climate shift.

Classroom climate refers to *the learning-related atmosphere* in a class. Simply put, it is a collection of expectations, shared by the teacher and the students, about *what kind of learning* is supposed to take place and *how* that learning will take place. So that's what classroom climate is. The second half of our two-part question is, "Why should teachers mess around with it?" The answer to this question is quite straightforward. *Appropriate classroom atmospheres benefit students*—both in their improved learning and in the kinds of affective dispositions they acquire.

The Shift Usually Sought

What sort of shift in classroom climate would a formatively inclined teacher ordinarily want to bring about? Well, given that different teachers generate different variations of classroom atmosphere, there is no single answer to this question. But, in general, teachers who vigorously apply the formative assessment process to their own teaching tend to move *away from a traditional classroom climate* and *toward an assessment-informed classroom climate.*

This is because the teacher's skillful use of classroom assessment fuels all the key learning-related decisions made in that classroom, including student conduct. This kind of shift from "traditional" to "test-illuminated" is a profound one.

Three Key Dimensions of an Assessment-Informed Classroom Climate

In *TA1*, I identified three prominent dimensions of classroom climate as the pivotal factors a teacher should focus on in order to promote a desirable classroom climate shift. Those three dimensions were (1) *learning expectations,* (2) *responsibility for learning,* and (3) *the role of classroom assessment.* The "before and after" characteristic of the shifts I advocated are summed up in Figure 8.1.

Learning expectations. Too often in a traditional classroom setting, the assumption is that academic success is only in the cards for students who happened to be "born smart" and who are academically motivated. Students who did not get so lucky in the gene-pool lottery, or students who prioritize other pursuits over studying hard and getting *A*s, tend to be written off—by both teachers and the students themselves—as unlikely to demonstrate high-level achievement. This is not the case in a "Level 3" or "assessment-informed" classroom. There, the expectation from students and definitely from the teacher is that *every student,* not just some, can—and will—learn, meet standards, and be successful.

Responsibility for learning. In a typical classroom, the teacher is regarded as the person who is predominantly responsible for kids' learning. I remember well from my own years as a student that there was no doubt about who was responsible for learning in almost every one of my classes. It was, without a whimper of an argument, most definitely *the teacher.*

Yet the kind of classroom climate foreseen in this application of formative assessment calls for a substantial shift in everyone's perception regarding who is truly responsible for learning. Although the teacher will always have a major responsibility for what students

FIGURE 8.1

Key Characteristics of a Classroom Climate Shift

	From		To
Learning Expectations	Substantial learning will occur for motivated students who possess adequate academic aptitude.	→	Substantial learning will occur for all students, irrespective of their academic aptitude.
Responsibility for Learning	The teacher, as prime instructional mover, is chiefly responsible for students' learning.	→	Students assume meaningful responsibility for their own learning and the learning of their classmates.
Role of Classroom Assessment	Formal tests generate data for comparing students and assigning grades.	→	Formal and informal assessments generate data for informing adjustments to the teacher's instruction and the students' learning tactics.

learn, it is imperative that students take on a substantial responsibility for their own learning and, ideally, for the learning of their classmates, as well.

Role of classroom assessment. In a traditional classroom, testing is seen as a way of comparing students and assigning grades. Testing is also used as a motivator, as when a teacher tells students to "Study hard, so you'll do well on the upcoming test!" But in the kind of classroom sought in this application of formative assessment, testing doesn't do either of these things. Rather, it provides the evidence both the teacher and the students use to make decisions about how to improve learning.

In the classroom climate we're talking about here, tests are rarely used to supply grades to students. Instead, they are employed to help teachers decide about instructional adjustments and to help students recognize their own strengths and weaknesses. Students' identified strengths can be used to help other students; their identified weaknesses can be tackled directly by the teacher, worked on individually by the student, and dealt with supportively by other students who can bring their strengths to a variety of peer-teaching activities. Because clarity and useful application is the endgame, descriptive feedback is preferred to number grades. Such descriptive feedback identifies the nature of the test-taker's difficulties and, whenever possible, suggests what might be done to overcome them. (If official regulations require a teacher to assign test-based grades to students, then all the teacher needs to do is inform students that an upcoming test will, of necessity, be graded. Such tests can be identified by a teacher as being externally imposed and not, in any meaningful way, part of the usual focus on improved learning.)

How to Shift Classroom Climate

Back in Chapter 1, I contended that this final application of formative assessment actually represented a *consummate implementation* of formative assessment. I really think it is. I should confess, however, that I simply adore the adjective "consummate," so I try to use it in almost anything I write—whether it fits or not. But in this instance it actually works well, because my dictionary's first definition of *consummate* is "complete or perfect." And this is precisely what the final application of formative assessment is—a complete and perfect implementation of the essential ingredients of the formative assessment process.

Implementing this application of formative assessment satisfactorily requires the use of one or more of the *teacher*-focused uses of formative assessment described in this book (Applications 1, 2, and 3) and the use of the *student*-focused use of formative assessment (Application 4) explored in Chapter 7. In short, for this final formative assessment application to have a reasonable chance of being successful, there must be a meaningful attempt to foster assessment-based adjustment decisions on the part of both the teacher and the teacher's students.

Unlike the previous chapters, in which a series of choice-points was set forth for each application, you'll find no parade of choice-points in this chapter. This is because what's going on in this application of formative assessment involves a straightforward theft of other applications. If, for instance, when trying to bring about a classroom climate shift, a teacher decided to use both Application 2 (focused on near-future instructional adjustments) and Application 4 (focused on students' learning tactic adjustments), then the teacher would need to address the choice-points listed in Chapters 5 and 7, respectively.

Another thing you won't find in this chapter are research-corroborated guidelines for how teachers should go about altering their classroom climates. The reason for that is simple: Such guidelines simply do not exist. Given the diversity of our schools and the often idiosyncratic array of instructional situations that exist within them, there is no definitive cookbook for classroom climate shifting. But that's no reason for me not to offer my own opinions, based on the teachers I've spoken with and the inspiring classrooms I've seen, regarding how a teacher who wants to try this application of formative assessment ought to go about it.

The first step for this teacher is to decide what he or she personally regards as the attributes that should account for a formatively-focused classroom climate. Many of the teachers I've spoken with hold to the dimensions set forth in Figure 8.1, but individual teachers —you, perhaps—might have different priorities. The question to ask is, *"What factors do I see as making the most difference in establishing the kind of classroom climate I want to have?"* It's best to keep the number of climate dimensions reasonably small, or you're apt to end up overwhelming yourself.

Then, either using the three dimensions recommended here, the dimensions you think most significant, or a blend of those dimensions, simply set out a plan to tackle each of the dimensions chosen. Perhaps you'll take only one action per dimension; perhaps you'll take more. But what's most necessary is that, for each attribute of classroom climate you regard as significant, you must make one or more deliberate moves to bring about a shift.

Because classroom climate is so dependent on students' affect, especially students' attitudes toward how learning is supposed to be taking place, I believe the affect-modification tactics identified in Chapter 7—modeling, reinforcement, and contiguity—have special relevance when a teacher decides to engage in any climate-shifting. But, whether you opt to use those affect-influencing techniques or decide on your own procedures, the most important thing is that you *do something.* That is, you take some action to try to bring about a shift in classroom climate, a shift toward an assessment-illuminated orientation to improved student learning.

Once of you have a plan sketched out, implement your actions and then monitor the payoffs of those actions. *TA1* provided a self-report affective inventory (Popham, 2008, pp. 106–107) that you might use on a pre/post basis to help determine if these desired shifts in climate are occurring.

We can now consider one approach to the climate-shifting fifth application of formative assessment. We'll be looking in on the classroom of a fictional teacher who has the luxury of working with colleagues who share the same mind-set regarding the benefits of the formative assessment process and the payoffs for students whose classroom climate has been thoughtfully altered.

In the Classroom

Marian Cory teaches 6th graders in a suburban school district in the southwest. She's been teaching for five years, and the last three of those years have been at Florence Adams School, a K–6 school chiefly serving children of middle-class families. The demographics of her school district have been relatively constant for the past decade, and the principal of Florence Adams School, Dr. Nadine Evans, has held this leadership post for the past six years. Marian's fellow teachers have immense respect for Dr. Evans, whose enthusiasm for the school's instructional efforts is contagious.

What sets Florence Adams School apart from the other district schools—and it is definitely regarded by other teachers in the district as a "different" kind of school—is its staff's commitment to what they refer to as a Constant Learning Climate (CLC)—an attempt to use formative assessment as the basis for a collaborative learning climate in each of the school's classrooms. All of the school's teachers meet every other Thursday afternoon to discuss and build on the CLC efforts. They've been meeting like this for years, originally as part of a professional development initiative supported by district funds, but continuing the effort on their own when the funds dried up.

Dr. Evans routinely attends these CLC meetings, where, more often than not, the attention falls on various teachers' efforts to improve their students' learning. Data is a big deal in these meetings—assessment data, to be specific. Clear, if slightly revised, echoes of the catchphrase from the movie *Jerry Maguire* ring out with regularity: "Show us the evidence!" these teachers say to one another.

The staff is preoccupied with establishing climates of collaboration in every single classroom, starting with kindergarten. It's an instructional and classroom management approach in which all students play an active role—not only in adjusting their own learning tactics, but in helping their classmates learn.

Several weeks ago, a 6th grader named Larry Bliss transferred into the school and into Marian's class, thereby bringing her enrollment up to 27 students. Two weeks after Larry's arrival, his father, Tony Bliss, made an appointment with Dr. Evans, the school's principal, to learn more about "the kind of instruction going on in Larry's classroom." In the meeting, Dr. Evans commented that it was understandable for Larry to be a bit confused about their CLC way of doing things, and she patiently explained the program's rationale. Mr. Bliss remained skeptical. He asked the principal's permission to sit in on his son's class so he could better understand the nature of this "very unusual 'learning climate' business." After a quick call on the intercom to Marian, the plans were set. Next Tuesday, Tony Bliss would spend the entire day watching Marian teach her 6th grade class.

Key Classroom Events

On that Tuesday, having introduced himself to Marian, Mr. Bliss took a seat in the back of his son's class, smiled briefly at Larry, and tried to be as unobtrusive as possible. He did, however, take notes throughout the entire day, leaving the classroom only when the students did so, and spending lunchtime sitting with two teachers in the school's cafeteria in order to get their comments on "this Constant Learning Climate."

The main thing Mr. Bliss noticed about his son's class was that it was so very different than any classes he had personally experienced when he was a student. For one thing, Marian was not a dominant—or even a clearly central—player in classroom events. For another, the students were particularly active. On at least three occasions during the day (in the math lesson, science lesson, and social studies lesson, to be specific), students independently configured themselves in different groups and worked together in clusters of four to six students. So far as Mr. Bliss could determine, certain students in these groups were functioning as tutors, while other students were serving as their tutees. Marian circulated around the classroom during these group tutorial sessions to answer students' questions, but the bulk of the "teaching" was coming from the *students,* not the teacher. Mr. Bliss noticed, too, that for some of these group tutorial sessions, the students who were tutees in one subject served as tutors in another subject. At points during the tutorial sessions, Marian simply sat at her desk. She seemed to be correcting papers, but Mr. Bliss wasn't sure. Although the noise level in the class was, in Mr. Bliss's view, occasionally too loud, he noted the students were talking almost exclusively about the subject matter.

In the middle of the math section that day, Marian asked her students to use their letter cards, and they immediately took out a set of index cards from their desks on which were printed, in very large and very black type, the letters A, B, C, and D. At that point, Marian asked the entire class a series of 10 questions, all of which seemed to be focused on the same geometry topic, although Mr. Bliss was not quite sure about this. For some questions, Marian sketched a geometric shape on the chalkboard. After Marian had read a question and its four potential answers aloud—and she always did so twice—she would then tell students, "Cards up!" Students would then show the letter card of their answers, Marian would scan the room to see what sorts of answers were being given, then she would say, "Cards down!" and make a few notes in a notepad before moving on to the next question. At the close of this letter-card quiz, Marian announced that, based on the quiz, she was going to lengthen the day's math period and deal again with a particular geometry principle. "Apparently, I have not taught this one well enough," she said. "There were five questions dealing with this principle on our little quiz, and on three of those five questions, I saw too many incorrect responses." She continued by explaining to students that this was another example of "how *my* instructional adjustments are based on *your* assessment results."

At the end of the add-on instruction about the geometry principle, Marian distributed a five-item practice quiz to the students. "Now, I'd like you, please, to answer all five items in the next few minutes, exchange papers with your math scoring partner, and then score the papers based on a scoring key that I'll pass out." After the practice quiz and paper-scoring swap was complete, the teacher made this request: "Please take a good look at your own score, and ask yourself if there's something you might want to change about how you're trying to learn this principle." She suggested to her students that, later in the day, when the "learning tactics" subgroup was scheduled to meet, students might wish to spend a few moments with that subgroup to help determine whether an adjustment in their learning tactics was indeed appropriate and, if so, what that adjustment might be.

Mr. Bliss captured most of these events in his notes, and he closed out his note taking with a particularly emphatic comment to his son: "Larry, this is most definitely not your daddy's school!"

The Interview of Marian Cory

by Parent Tony Bliss

Thanks so very much, Ms. Cory, for letting me watch what you were doing for Larry and his classmates. And thanks also for this interview time. I know you must be busy. And after watching you and your students for an entire day, I am sure you'll need to get ready for tomorrow, so I promise to be brief. I just had no idea what to make of this Constant Learning Climate business. I know for certain that Larry has never had anything like it in his two previous schools.

Well, in that regard, Mr. Bliss, I was just like Larry when I joined this school's faculty three years ago. I'd never seen anything like CLC— as either a teacher or when I was a student myself. So I certainly understand why you might want to look in on Larry's class. Actually, our principal, Dr. Evans, works hard to get more parents to drop in on their children's classes. It's wonderful that you found a way to spend an entire day at the school. Now, what specific questions do you have about what you saw?

I guess my first question deals with those occasions, I think you called them "adjustment opportunities," that you gave to the students—and to yourself when you did the letter-card quiz on geometry and the follow-up five-question quiz. It seems you were deciding whether to change what you were doing. And you gave the students a chance to change what they were doing. Is providing adjustment opportunities like this a central part of the CLC program?

It is! Making adjustment opportunities a pivotal part of this approach makes it clear to students that we, the teachers, aren't asking of them any more than we ask of ourselves. We want students to monitor their own ways of trying to learn, and we monitor our own ways of trying to teach. If we can convince our students that we're all in this together, and that they too have a personal responsibility for learning things as well as they can, then we think students will develop better attitudes toward schooling.

But how do you know when to have students monitor their own learning techniques or, for that matter, when to monitor your own instruction?

That's an excellent question. At this school, our entire approach to education is closely allied with what is generally referred to as "formative assessment." It's an instructional approach that relies heavily on the use of classroom assessments. Those assessments—and you saw several different sorts of classroom assessments today—produce the evidence that allows both teachers *and* students to make better decisions about what, if anything, to adjust about their teaching or their learning.

In my classroom, and throughout the building, we rely on what are referred to as "learning progressions." A learning progression is simply a set of carefully sequenced "building blocks" that we believe students must first master if they are going to be successful in mastering a more distant curricular target, such as an important skill or a body of knowledge. Most of us try to collect assessment evidence from students toward the end of the time that we instructionally address each of the building blocks in a learning progression. This is what I was doing today in that math segment dealing with geometry.

Where do these learning progressions come from? Does each teacher create his or her own learning progressions?

Several of the teachers in this school create their learning progressions solo. And they're quite good at it. But most of the learning progressions we rely on were created collaboratively by members of our faculty—sometimes with the assistance of a district curriculum specialist. Creating a learning progression requires good, hard thinking, and it helps to enlist the efforts of numerous teachers.

Tell me about those tutorial groups. I've never seen students engage so actively and so seriously in teaching other students. Do all the teachers in the school use these sorts of groups?

As it turns out, most of our teachers do set up these sorts of peer-teaching models. In my class, they seem to work well, and what I like about them is that students can shift roles based on what their assessment results tell them. A student might be a tutor in one subject and receive tutoring in another. I don't know if your son told you, but just last week, Larry became a tutor in one of our language arts tutorial groups.

Yeah, you know, he did mention it, but without any context, I really didn't know what he meant. So, how common is this approach, Ms. Cory? Have you taught in another school with the same emphasis on this kind of learning climate?

This is my first experience with such a program, Mr. Bliss. There's no question that Dr. Evans, our principal, makes all the difference here. Without her constant support, I don't know if this approach would survive. I hope it would, but she's so supportive, and she makes sure we teachers get plenty of professional development time.

I'll also tell you, quite frankly, that if the other teachers in the school were not committed to the CLC approach, I don't think I could use it as successfully as I do. You saw how I try to teach Larry and his 26 classmates. Just imagine how difficult it would be for me to try to introduce this "shared responsibility" kind of learning on my own, after my students had spent kindergarten through 5th grade in a more traditional teacher-centered classroom. To me, it seems that this particular way of using formative assessment as the foundation for instruction demands a commitment from *all* the teachers in a school—or at least almost all of them.

Larry, of course, is a transfer student, but he is surrounded by wonderful role models in my other students. They've been through many years of CLC here at Florence Adams. It won't take your son long to catch on completely. I'm sure you'll find that, by the end of the school year, our school's embrace of formative assessment will have been wonderful for Larry's learning and, perhaps more importantly, for the way in which Larry regards himself as a learner.

An Interview Look-Back

During this interview, Larry's father raised the issues of most concern to him, and they were important issues. Mr. Bliss was unfamiliar with an approach to instruction oriented around the use of formative assessment, and this raises a point worth considering by all teachers who might wish to install one or more variants of the formative assessment process. It is likely that formative assessment practices will be genuinely unfamiliar to most parents, a reality that supports the wisdom of proactively informing parents of how it works, how it will affect classroom practices, and how it is likely to benefit student learning.

A classroom climate shift calls for students to become actively involved in monitoring their own progress and in helping other students make progress. Mr. Bliss saw this in action when the tutorial group work got under way. Note, though, that although research reviews such as the Black and Wiliam analysis (1998) support formative assessment's effectiveness in helping students learn, there is no current research to support the notion that any specific pedagogical techniques for implementing formative assessment—ways of collecting evidence, for example, or the decisions that a teacher might make in response to performance data—are clearly superior to any others. However, we can say that Marian Cory's decision to have her students self-select into peer-tutoring groups, for example, seems like a reasonable instructional adjustment.

One final issue worth calling to your attention deals with Marian's apprehension about her chances of making this particular instructional approach work in a school where there weren't so many other teachers employing the same formative assessment strategies. There is no current evidence regarding what constitutes the minimal level of staff commitment required to make this approach work, and there probably never will be, but there is considerable cogency in Marian's concern.

If you are a teacher who is giving serious consideration to trying a classroom climate shift, it is certainly possible to proceed unilaterally in your school. And you certainly might be successful. However, if you can install this instructional change at the same time that other teachers in your school are doing so, you'll surely find the going much easier.

Reflection Questions

1. If you were advising a colleague on how to establish this application of formative assessment and promote a successful shift to an assessment-informed classroom climate, what instructional or classroom organizational moves would you recommend. Why?

2. How would you rank the relative importance of the three dimensions of classroom climate addressed in this chapter: *learning expectations, responsibility for learning,* and *the role of classroom assessment*? Would a teacher ever want to leave any of these dimensions unaddressed when promoting a shift in classroom climate? Why or why not?

3. Do you think it is possible for a teacher to bring about a classroom climate shift via full-blown formative assessment when all other teachers in that school are satisfied with a more traditional kind of classroom climate? Why or why not? What factors would support the success of a teacher who is "going it alone" in efforts to promote the adoption of an assessment-informed classroom climate?

4. Examine a lesson you currently teach and map out how you might conduct it in an assessment-informed classroom climate. What variation of teacher-focused formative assessment might you use? (Remember, you'll need at least one.) How might you employ student-focused formative assessment?

9

Reports From the Field

As soon as ASCD agreed to publish this sequel to *Transformative Assessment,* I decided it would be great if I could get actual users of formative assessment to contribute a set of commentaries representing the flavor of what goes on inside classrooms when the process is in full flower. Accordingly, I contacted several teachers I'd met during workshops, but mostly I relied on the recommendations of five friends, identified in the Acknowledgments, who gave me the names of two dozen educators they regarded as stellar users of formative assessment.

Almost every invited educator sent me something. If, after reading what these educators wrote, you don't find yourself personally motivated to get formative assessment used more widely in our schools, then you really should reread this chapter's commentaries —this time, paying closer attention!

A number of these testimonials contain content ideally suited to further consideration during the deliberations of a professional learning community (PLC) dealing with applications of the formative assessment process. If you are a member of such a PLC, as you read, try to identify topics or procedures used by those teachers that you think warrant further scrutiny by you and your PLC colleagues.

I've taken the liberty of titling all of these 18 mini-essays and introducing each one with a few comments. I am, as you might infer, genuinely grateful to the educators who were willing to share their views of formative assessment with you and me. In no particular order, then, let's see what some real users of formative assessment have to say about it.

A Bridge to the Miraculous

Here's a teacher for whom formative assessment has become far more than a once-in-a-while testing technique employed to monitor his students' progress. When I read Robert Callahan's comments, I'm struck by the central and pervasive role formative assessment plays in his instructional decision making. Moreover, because his conception of teaching is infinitely more ambitious than merely covering curricular content, Robert clearly needs a toolbox suitable for taking him to those heights. He appears to have found one.

Here's what I think teachers do. We start with hope, a very simple hope. It's the hope that we can help, truly help, a student learn something useful, valuable, empowering, inspiring. We build an image of that something. Maybe we start with a prestated objective or a couple of pages from the text or the basic joy we, ourselves, feel when we read, write, think, and solve.

The hope leads to searching. How can I build a lesson that will engage the learner? Where will I begin? What are the guideposts that will tell me what to do? I want this instruction to work. How will I know that it is working?

Formative assessment is my bridge to the miraculous. Learning progressions pave the pragmatic road I travel. Student responses on whiteboards are my guideposts. Traffic signals—the stacks of red, yellow, and green cups students keep on their desk and use to convey their understanding—are the immediate link between the students and me. This is the voice they use to guide my lessons.

Formative assessment is my universal toolbox for teaching. It reminds me to be clever, humble, thoughtful, kind, and wise in the presence of learning. It is the reference point that allows me to reflect and decide what is the best thing to do next . . . and now. . . and now.

Robert Callahan
6th Grade Teacher
Emma Wilson Elementary School
Chico, California

One Announcement, One Changed Teacher

Never underestimate the impact that your comments may have on the conduct of your colleagues. Here we have some comments from Jill Rodgers, an elementary school teacher who heard a veteran educator proclaim formative assessment to be an instructional game-changer. As it happened, Jill was looking for some changes and decided to give the process a try. The outcome was everything she'd hoped for and more.

A couple years into teaching, I attended a conference that focused, in part, on formative assessment. A gentleman stood up, announced that he was a veteran teacher of more than 30 years, and said formative assessment practices had changed everything he knew about teaching and had made a great impact in his classroom. That got my attention. I was looking for a shift in my classroom—a new direction that would get my students more involved in their learning. Maybe there really was something to this formative assessment.

Soon, I experienced the power of formative assessment for myself. I saw what can happen when ongoing assessment guides planning, teaching, student participation, and learning. Maybe the most striking thing is how the classroom dynamic changes. We started as a classroom of 1 teacher and 27 students, and became a culture of 28 teachers and 28 learners, all with individual strengths, all able to assist one another, and all with the *desire* to assist one another.

I created clear learning targets and set up ways for my 4th and 5th graders to monitor their own progress. Self-assessment gave students a way to articulate their successes and their needs, and I was able to use their self-supplied information, coupled with my own observations, to form differentiated groups for reteaching, practice, or extensions. I also changed my attitude toward grading. I realized it was not so important to grade everything—to give students a mark, letter, or number. The benefit of looking at students' work is to gain information from it. What did the student do well? What did the student need to work on? Were there other students in the class who had the same needs? How could I adjust my instructional plans to reflect this reality? Once the students and I had set up this environment, they were naturally ready for goal setting, as they could see that goals were an extension of individual needs.

I knew my formative assessment efforts were becoming successful when I witnessed the massive change in student attitudes. There was no longer any mystery about what needed to be learned, how to learn it, or even what "proficiency" looked like. Students took ownership of their learning, and motivation shot through the roof. I started hearing an increase in academic language as students began vocalizing their awareness of proficiency in certain areas. With this came a comfort in knowing that every child now had the confidence to ask for help and to assist others. Every child seemed to grasp that there was not just one way, or one time, to prove mastery; they could do it at any time. When students started sacrificing their recesses to show me proficiency on learning targets, I knew authentic learning was happening right before my eyes.

Jill Rodgers
4th/5th Grade Teacher
Hodgkins Elementary School
Denver, Colorado

A Middle School Teacher's Commemorative

Lorraine Sprout, the veteran Vermont middle school teacher who wrote this next commentary, did not live to see it in its published version. I think you'll agree that Lorraine's words here clearly communicate the sense the excitement that formative assessment brought to her teaching. She will be missed.

In my 27 years of teaching, primarily at the 7th and 8th grade levels, I have tried one "new and exciting" way of teaching adolescents after another, and each of these strategies only lasted until something else "new and exciting" came along. Then, three years ago, I was introduced to formative assessment. I read a little about it, and some of my colleagues took part in a formative assessment training session; their enthusiasm intrigued me. I visited some classrooms where teachers were using this "new and exciting" program and found myself caught up in the best educational experience that I had ever encountered.

For me, the most significant outcome of formative assessment is the way that it helps students become aware of, concerned with, and responsible for their own learning. The "fun" parts of formative assessment (traffic signaling, creating student-made rubrics, and so on) are far more than just entertaining. They give quick, honest feedback on where the students' understanding levels are, who is ready to move on, and who needs a bit or a great deal of help. This makes grouping for instruction focused on a specific skill or concept much more effective. It also supports differentiated education, which is sacred in our school—and rightfully so.

I am a "graying teacher," as those of us with many years of experience are often labeled. Formative assessment startled me from complacency and has made coming to school every morning as exciting as it was 27 years ago.

Lorraine Sprout
Middle School Teacher
The St. Johnsbury School
St. Johnsbury, Vermont

English Language Learners and a "Culture of Learning"

The research supporting formative assessment's virtues is wide-ranging, with positive effects documented for students of all ages, from very young children to graduate students, and in classes covering a wide array of subjects. And, as middle school teacher Sarah Metzler describes, formative assessment was just the thing for engaging her difficult-to-reach students. She notes that it was "a great fit" for her situation. Odds are that in most other teaching situations, it will fit equally well.

As a teacher of English Language Learners (ELLs), I knew that my students' learning needed to be meaningful, appropriate, attainable, and highly scaffolded. But keeping students engaged was not always easy. My ELL students were easily frustrated by what they didn't know and by how hard it could be to move forward. Traditional teaching methods were not cutting it.

I discovered that formative assessment was a great fit for my situation, and the more I use it, the more engaged my students become. Formative assessment allows them to have more involvement in the actual learning process at every step of our lessons. All students benefit from knowing *why* they need to do something and, if the path is obvious, the learning is much more relevant. They have more buy-in, and this ultimately leads to greater success.

I like to begin units by giving students a pre-test to determine what they already know. This helps them focus on the subject matter and set goals about how they can master the areas where they are not as strong. I want to help them feel successful in what they already *can* do while giving them a real picture of what lies ahead and what else they need to know to achieve the final learning objective. Progress monitoring, goal setting, and peer assessment give students the chance to take responsibility for moving themselves forward by building on their prior skills and knowledge.

My ELL students do so much better now that the learning environment is set up in a way that makes sense to them. They know that everything they are doing in class has been planned to help them demonstrate what they know. This kind of planning keeps their levels of understanding visible to me, and I can go on to adjust my instruction to address their specific needs.

I still have a lot to learn about formative assessment, and it isn't always easy to give up the traditional concepts of teaching. But the more I use formative assessment, the more I am convinced that it is a crucial part of creating a true culture of learning.

Sarah Metzler
ELL Teacher (Grades 6–8)
Shaw Heights Middle School
Westminster, Colorado

Formative Assessment as Transformative?

We now hear not from a teacher, but from a coordinator of professional development. Yes, even school administrators occasionally have sensible things to say! This administrator, Beth Cobb, describes leading her school's professional development about formative assessment as the "most exciting" work she's done as an educator, remarking on both the difference formative assessment has made in the way her school's teachers plan for instruction and the positive ways in which it's altered grading practices.

Over a period of four years, I have seen formative assessment transform the instruction at our school. Honestly, leading our school's professional development focused on formative assessment has been the most exciting work that I have been involved in as an educator. When teachers are willing to tackle formative assessment and try some of its strategies and tactics in their classrooms, they become energized by what they learn from their students. It is exciting to speak with teachers as they reflect on their changes in instruction.

The difference, as I've seen it, is that teachers plan differently when using formative assessment. Integrating formative assessment throughout the lesson gives them a better understanding of where their students are as learners, and they are able differentiate their instruction more effectively.

These days in our school, I hear teachers having conversations in the hallways about learning intentions and exit tickets. Students ask teachers for the learning intention if it is not posted. They want to know what is expected of them. I often meet with teachers to look at a lesson's exit tickets to see whether or not the students actually met the predetermined learning intention. We discuss the direction of the next lesson, as informed by the evidence on students' exit tickets.

This transforming of instruction and learning is clearly displayed in classrooms. It is exciting to see students taking ownership of their own learning. Because they know the success criteria, they can self-assess their own work and assess the work of their peers.

With student self-assessment and peer assessment now the norm at our school, teachers spend less time "grading" and more time giving effective written feedback. Formative assessment has also driven us to a standards-based report card. Letter grades no longer work for us. As teachers put it, "How can we settle for average-based grades when students show progress throughout the term?" They know the real story is whether students have met the standards, the feedback on learning that teachers and students get throughout the term, and the adjustments they make in response to meet those standards. If I had to say it in one sentence, I'd say that the implementation of formative assessment has transformed our school.

Beth Cobb
Coordinator of Professional Development
The St. Johnsbury School
St. Johnsbury, Vermont

Focused Lessons, Reflective Learners, and Failure as a Thing of the Past

When teachers get serious about giving formative assessment a whirl in their classrooms, the effects of that choice can sometimes be surprising. For example, after implementing formative assessment, our next contributor, mathematics support teacher Melanie Cifonelli, realized she could no longer plan her instruction around "the great activity" and then ferret out a learning goal that seems to mesh with it. What I find most affecting in this piece, though, is Melanie's regret related to those students she taught before she embraced formative assessment. However, Melanie believes that when students realize what they need to do to be successful during every lesson—and receive the right kind of support—failure will evaporate.

During my 21 years as an educator, I have been trained on many different district initiatives. Two years ago, I began an in-depth study of formative assessment in the classroom, and this study has had the most profound effect on several dimensions of my teaching: how I plan and implement lessons, how I think about my content, how I think about grading students, and how I involve students in the work they do together and on their own. I want to talk first about planning. Thanks to formative assessment, my lessons are much more focused and targeted for specific goals than they've ever been. Today, when I plan a lesson, I am usually planning for at least three opportunities to find out what my students know, what misconceptions they may be holding onto, and where individual students are in their learning progression. Now that I do this, every lesson has a clear purpose, and I no longer find myself guessing where my instruction should go next. When I am planning, I come up with questions and activities designed to elicit information on student progress toward their learning goals—information I will use to provide truly helpful feedback that will move students forward. I now search for the activity that matches the lesson goal instead of starting with "the great activity" and looking for a goal that suits it.

Writing specific goals instead of behavioral objectives has helped me think much more deeply about the content I am teaching. I must ask myself why I am teaching a lesson, what kind of thinking I want my students to do, and what connections or generalizations I want my students to make. Because I know that part of formative assessment is sharing learning goals with my students, I must be sure that the goals I choose are meaningful, appropriate, and truly target exactly what I want my students to know and be able to do. The process of determining learning goals and building learning progressions has enhanced my content knowledge and process knowledge in such a way that I feel much more confident giving next-step feedback to students.

The main reason I use formative assessment is because I believe when it is used consistently and well, students become engaged, self-reflective, and self-motivated learners. I cringe when I think about the hours I spent grading papers only to watch students toss those papers into the recycling bin without a second glance. I want to cry when I think of the numbers of students who have walked out of my classroom not "making the grade" and not understanding what they did wrong on the assignment or how to correct their mistakes.

My experience with formative assessment has taught me that when students know what they need do to be successful during every lesson, and when they know that the teacher is constantly looking for their feedback, they will rise to the high standards that are set. Formative assessment *will* work when there is this kind of give-and-take relationship between the students and teacher, as well as within the class itself. I firmly believe it will give rise to a new generation of students who are not afraid to admit that they do not know everything; who see learning as adventure, not as a chore; and who understand that with the right kind of guidance and support, they can achieve any goal.

Melanie Cifonelli

Instructional Support Teacher for Mathematics, Grades 6–8,
Clary & Blodgett School
Syracuse, New York

Exit Tickets Instead of Crystal Balls

Sixth grade mathematics teacher Matthew Hoover confesses that one of his most difficult tasks is accurately discerning what his students are thinking. He uses exit tickets or, as he describes them, "tickets out of the door" as a formative assessment evidence-gathering technique, and appears to be pleased with it. What's clear from his commentary is that he makes certain the questions he uses for his exit tickets, insofar as is possible, give him a realistic estimate regarding the proportion of his students who appear to be mastering the learning goal he has set for that day. Compared with a crystal ball, Matt's assessment ploy seems far more defensible.

For me, one of the most challenging aspects of teaching is figuring out what students are thinking. In my classroom, formative assessment has provided me with a window into my students' thought processes. I use the knowledge I gain to guide my instruction and to individualize it to better meet each of my students' needs.

One of my favorite formative assessment strategies is the exit card or "ticket out of the door." I use this strategy when I need a quick assessment of what students have taken from a daily lesson. This "ticket out of the door" can be one or more questions or problems that will give me a quick look at how many of my students met the learning goal or goals I set for that day. If the ticket data tell me that many members of the class are falling short, then I will reteach the lesson within a day or two, revising it based on what I've learned. If I notice that only a few students are not meeting the goal, I usually pull them aside the next day and instruct them as a small group. It's an environment in which I can find out more about what they are thinking, and I can target any misconceptions on an individual basis.

Matthew Hoover
Mathematics Teacher, 6th Grade
Shumate Middle School
Gibraltar, Michigan

Targeting Students' Learning Needs, Not Teachers' Teaching Needs

Mathematics support teacher Shawn Morgan employs formative assessment to ensure he aims his instruction at what his students need rather than at what he might want to show them. As he notes in this commentary, Shawn spent a good many years being frustrated by his students' lack of success, and his monitoring of student progress only showed him how limited that progress generally was. But then he embraced formative assessment, and struggling students began to "make real, measurable gains."

I use formative assessment because it helps me provide my students with instruction that is targeted toward exactly what they need in order to move forward in their learning. Before formative assessment, I primarily used unit tests and weekly quizzes as my source of data to monitor student progress. I would record the grades and move on with the curriculum—knowing in the back of my mind that many of my students were not ready to be successful in the next unit. Relying on such summative assessments as unit tests and quizzes to monitor progress did not meet the needs of my students. If anything, it led to student frustration, as they consistently struggled to grasp concepts. I was frustrated, too, because these same students kept failing over and over, despite my best efforts to reach them. It was clear that I was using the wrong approach and, unfortunately, this pattern continued for many years until I started to learn about and to use formative assessment.

Formative assessment taught me how I could meet the needs of all of my students. Once I began to infuse it into my daily teaching, I was able to identify the misconceptions and learning gaps in the moment and make informed decisions about future instruction. I found myself listening and responding to what my students were telling and showing me instead of focusing on what *I* wanted to tell and show *them*. The way I monitored progress changed as well. Instead of relying solely on numbers that told what my students had learned over a large chunk of time, I was relying on notes and narratives that focused on what they were learning in real time. The final product became less important than the actual process my students were using to produce it. Students who had typically struggled and made limited progress in my class started to make real, measurable gains. I could honestly begin to say that my classroom had become a place where all students could learn and achieve success.

Shawn Morgan
Mathematics Instructional Support Teacher
Dr. John Van Duyn Elementary and H. W. Smith Schools
Syracuse, New York

Formative Assessment and Struggling Students

Rachel Lambrix-Hoover is a 6th grade English/Language Arts teacher, and one of the classes she teaches consists of 13 struggling students. What Rachel has discovered for herself is what the oft-cited research review by Paul Black and Dylan Wiliam (1998) explicitly states: Formative assessment functions particularly well with students who are experiencing learning difficulties. Her comments highlight formative assessment's power to inform effective differentiation.

Last January, I was given the opportunity to join a formative assessment team. I had heard the buzz about the effectiveness of using formative assessment in the classroom, and wanted to find out how I could become a great teacher, not just a good teacher. I attended a two-day workshop, and I was hooked.

I use formative assessment because I know it works. Every teacher wants to see his or her students succeed, and formative assessment helps me help my students achieve their academic goals. It has an especially huge effect on struggling students. When I see these once-frustrated kids succeed, I know that the effort formative assessment requires of me is truly worth it.

For example, I am currently teaching a class called "Academic Success," designed for students who need extra assistance in language arts. There are only 13 students in this class, so I am able to individualize instruction quite a bit. I begin a unit with a pre-assessment that covers each of the related grade-level expectations, and then use spreadsheet software to chart each student's scores and status. Our school is currently using a technology-based program that allows teachers to create assessments for individual students based on their individual needs. With the use of this technology, I am able to create new assessments for each student that include only questions related to that student's deficient areas. As the students master the concepts, their assessments keep pace. I also use the results over the course of the trimester to guide reteaching in small groups. I have long known that differentiating instruction for each student was important, but it's only now, with formative assessment giving me a clearer picture of my students' individual needs, that I am really seeing how powerful and effective differentiation can be.

Rachel Lambrix-Hoover
English/Language Arts Teacher
Shumate Middle School
Gibraltar, Michigan

What to Do When Students Are Awash?

One of the most difficult tasks for formatively oriented teachers is figuring out what to do when students trip an adjustment trigger. Here we learn how Karin Kirnie, a mathematics coach, faces this challenge. Note that Karin's approach involves having a few "go-to response strategies" when too many red cards rumble into view. In this commentary, Karin lays out some of her instructional repair strategies.

In my job as a math coach I've seen many teachers who have great mathematical knowledge. They stand up front and put on a great show. Several students do the head bob ("Yeah, yeah; I've got it!"). Those students might be the same ones who volunteer or yell out the answers. The teacher feels satisfied that the class has it and moves on, not realizing which students get it and which ones don't. But put in a simple formative assessment strategy, such as the use of thumbs-up/down or traffic-light cards, and that teacher will know immediately who has mastered a topic, who almost has it, and who doesn't have it at all.

"We didn't learn this last year!" How many times have you heard your students say that? And how many times has that led you to wonder just what last year's teachers were doing if they weren't teaching such-and-such basic skill? It's a question that becomes funny, painfully so, when you've switched grades, like I have, and know for a fact that *you* taught it to them last year.

Formative assessment shifts the locus of control for learning away from the teacher and toward the student. Students are the ones who tell you what they have mastered and what is still a struggle for them.

So you learn some useful student self-assessment strategies—traffic-light response cards, whiteboards, tickets-out-the-door—and you use them. You're gathering good data, good feedback from your students. But what you *do* with that feedback is the crux of the matter. What does your plan book look like? How do you keep your plans for the unit "on track" and deal with the red-card traffic signals telling you that students aren't picking up what you're putting down? It's essential to be prepared for adjustment, and I have a few go-to response strategies.

If I see a fair number of red cards—enough to trip my predetermined adjustment trigger, I might respond with an immediate adjustment of having students explain their reasoning to each other or I might, during the next class session, ask students to create a learning center focused on the topic in question. If the majority of my students are displaying red cards—way above my tipping point—then giving more instruction on the topic is often appropriate—as long as I'm careful not to present the material in the way I did before. This could mean unleashing new sets of examples (something I can do immediately) or taking a day or so to figure out a whole new approach. I'm also mindful that lots and lots of red cards may be an indication that students didn't understand the concepts that came *before* this lesson. Thus, knowing the learning progression is clearly essential.

Karin Kirnie
Mathematics Coach
Lincoln, Ed Smith, Frazer, and H. W. Smith Schools
Syracuse, New York

Even Mandates Can Have Happy Endings

Here we have a high school science teacher who took up formative assessment not because of scientific evidence, but because she was told to. Yet Kimberly Campbell soon discovered that, even though formative assessment had been administratively mandated, this assessment-abetted approach to instruction actually paid off for her students. What's especially intriguing about Kimberly's commentary is her rejection of certain oft-applauded formative assessment techniques and her meaningful modification of others. Because current research evidence indicates that there is no "one best way" to install formative assessment, this gives scientifically oriented teachers such as Kimberly a considerable range of implementation options. As long as the truly essential ingredients of formative assessment are in place, teachers can use a variety of procedures to make it purr.

Although my original beginnings with formative assessment were triggered by a mandate from the administration, I quickly discovered that this was not a program where you learned something and then set it aside. Formative assessment was something that not only made sense to use, but was also beneficial to my teaching.

It's always been routine for me to watch my students' faces to see if they seem to be getting what I'm presenting. And I'd also had them answer five questions before they left the classroom so I could discover what I needed to review the next day. Studying the formative assessment process gave me names for the things I was already doing, but it also provided numerous new things for me to try.

Some of these new formative assessment techniques were not compatible with either my teaching style or the subject I was teaching, so they did not work well. But when I found the methods that clicked for me within the current subject, and then applied them, and they worked with my students, I started looking for ways to use them more often. My favorite is something I modified from many of the ideas I was using. To help students become more responsible for their own learning, they keep a weekly learning journal in which they write down the "lesson question" I ask them each day, and provide an answer to it. They are allowed to help each other answer these questions daily. Then, at the end of the week, they have to write a summary of what they have learned that week at the top of the page and any questions they still have at the bottom. I review these responses over the weekend to see how well students are grasping the lesson and whether they possess the knowledge they need to move on with the topic. And I make sure to address these issues—and the questions they have—in the next week's instruction. What's interesting is that many students find through their summary that they can answer their own questions. And I can read their summaries to see if they possess the knowledge they need to move on with the topic. It has been an important tool for me, but it is invaluable to the students, who begin to see their learning as a progression over several weeks.

Overall, I guess I use formative assessment because it makes sense to figure out where my students are before I try to move them somewhere else. Everything from allowing them to participate in the process of rubric-writing to helping them come up with interesting ways of creating their class summaries gives order to their learning. Doing these things informally is a start, but coming up with ways for them to see how formative assessment works gives students daily ownership of their own education. And in the end, I believe this is what education is all about.

Kimberly Campbell
Science Teacher
Carver High School
Winston-Salem, North Carolina

Touching All the Bases

When baseball players hit a home run, they round the bases and "touch 'em all" on the way back to home plate. Well, when we hear about a school where so many enlightened formative assessment practices are taking place, it almost seems that the school's educators

*have, indeed, socked a formative assessment home run out of the
ballpark. In this commentary from an experienced school principal,
Marion Anastasia identifies an absolute flock of first-rate formative
assessment practices which support her claim of having a school that
is "learning centered." She and her colleagues have had four full years
of implementing formative assessment; I think they have definitely
earned the right to "touch 'em all!"*

From the perspective of a principal and former teacher, one of the
most compelling reasons a school should use formative assessment
is to transform its culture from one that is "teaching centered" to
one that is "learning centered." At our school, teachers recognized
this shift as an outcome from the last four years of implementing
formative assessment. Once teachers believed that teacher quality
is the single *most* influential factor in raising student achievement,
there was a clear shift in the school's culture, beliefs about learning,
shared leadership, and the changing role of teachers.

Both students and teachers hold each other accountable for the
learning that goes on in classrooms as well as in teacher learning
communities. In classrooms, clearly stated learning intentions and
success criteria are a "standard of practice" for every lesson, every
day. Given this, students know what they are learning and what it
looks like if they are successful. All students participate with the
expectation that they contribute to their own learning as well as to
that of their peers—no exceptions.

Students benefit from feedback techniques such as comment-
only marking, find-and-fix, and traffic signaling. These tactics
provide explicit direction so students can move learning forward.
Compare that with the implied finality of a letter grade. Deeper
thinking is fostered by high-quality questioning strategies, and all
students are expected to actively participate. I use popsicle stick
draws to elicit responses randomly. Therefore, equity of access to
rigorous, relevant questioning is ensured.

Teachers identify professional learning communities as an
essential support necessary to develop their practices. This is a

time for collegial support, as well as a time to take risks while sharing challenges and successes. The work in PLCs has renewed our teachers' passion for teaching! Shared leadership is cultivated as teachers take on roles as teacher-leaders to facilitate PLCs. Teachers are engaged in new learning as they identify innovative strategies and techniques to implement in their classrooms.

I can walk into any classroom (prekindergarten through grade 8) at any time of day, and whisper in a student's ear, "What are you learning?" Students always respond, with confidence, by clearly describing a learning intention that reflects a specific concept or skill. We believe all students and teachers can achieve. Formative assessment is our common ground; it has made our school a genuine community of learners.

Marion Anastasia
Principal
The St. Johnsbury School
St. Johnsbury, Vermont

Nurturing Learners Who Identify Their Own Needs

In this commentary we see the previously introduced Shawn Morgan employing traffic-signal cards in his mathematics instruction. What's particularly interesting in this case is Shawn's clear commitment to fostering students' ability to identify their own needs so they can then seek suitable support or instruction. He's working to sharpen students' metacognitive skills and support their evolution into autonomous learners.

As Margaret Heritage once told me, "It's not formative unless something is formed from it." In essence, until I make a decision about my future instruction that is based on what my students are producing in real time, it cannot be considered formative assessment.

One of my favorite formative assessment strategies is to engage my students in metacognitive responses. For example, I like to regularly stop student activity during a lesson and ask students to revisit the success criteria. Then I ask them to use a traffic-signal card to signify their progress relative to the success criteria. Red means "struggling," yellow means "some success," and green means "no problems." If I ask, they must be prepared to provide evidence that supports their choice. During these quick assessments, I am able to gather data that tells me how the class as a whole is feeling about their learning at that moment.

The data helps me quickly decide who can continue on to work independently, who I can intervene with immediately, who I will need to provide with targeted interventions at a later time, and who might need to be moved back in the learning progression to be better prepared to successfully satisfy this specific criterion. Although students can be hesitant with this approach at first, most come to find it rewarding. They quickly become proficient evaluators of their own progress. And they develop skills that allow them to become learners who can identify their own needs and seek the appropriate targeted support or instruction.

Shawn Morgan
Mathematics Instructional Support Teacher
Dr. John Van Duyn Elementary and H. W. Smith Schools
Syracuse, New York

Success with Inner-City Math Students

How well does formative assessment work in tough-to-teach settings? Well, here's a perspective from Sharon Pernisi, a middle school math teacher who taught inner-city 8th graders about the "majesty of mathematics" during a summer session. Talk about tough! But as Sharon found, the same process that gives her insight into student progress and leads her to refine her instruction also promotes the kind of student engagement, awareness, and motivation that is an additional and very powerful boost to learning.

Perhaps the best reason to use formative assessment in the classroom is to involve students in their own assessment process. In a classroom where formative assessment is present, the learning cycle is transparent to students. Teachers explicitly share and refer back to learning goals and success criteria, and students think metacognitively about their learning—there is no mystery. Students are in a partnership with teachers with regard to their learning. With this partnership comes shared motivation and responsibility for what transpires during a lesson.

I really put this theory of student involvement and self-assessment to the test in my inner-city 8th grade summer school math class. Most of the students were minorities who had been retained at least one grade in the past and could not go on to high school without showing minimum competency in math. The threat of another year in middle school was not as motivating as one might think. And most students were so close to the dropout age that summer school was more about the free breakfast and free lunch than it was about academics. So it was with this group of young men and women that I first used daily reflection on learning goals and success criteria.

Students would begin each class by recording their learning goal and success criteria in a reflection log. After discussing the goal and success criteria, and referring back to them several times throughout the lesson, students had to reflect in writing on how well they did reaching that day's goal. If they felt they met a goal or satisfied a success criterion, the evidence (classwork) was stapled to the reflection and placed in the student's portfolio. This was all student-directed. Students made decisions about whether a goal was reached and which piece of classwork served as evidence of reaching that learning goal. On Wednesdays and Fridays, students would have five-minute portfolio conferences with me. We would talk about the goals and criteria they'd met, and we'd devise a plan for the ones they did not meet, both in terms of what I could do for them instructionally and what they could do in terms of a learning adjustment.

At first, this was a very uncomfortable process for my students. They were very hesitant to believe that their input mattered. It was hard for them to develop a mind-set that they were partners with me in their learning process. Every time a student would ask me,

"Ms. Pernisi, am I passing?" I would say, "Go get your portfolio." We'd sit down together and go over the student's reflection on each learning goal and success criteria. After some discussion, I'd say, "So, are you passing?" I'd wait for them to answer the question based on the evidence, which was proof of learning. Then we'd talk about the pieces of the success criteria they still needed to work on. By the end of summer school, all of my students had an exit interview with me. Portfolios in hand, they were able to provide evidence of their learning. These students became motivated and involved in their learning process. I can't think of a better reason to use formative assessment.

Sharon L. Pernisi
Instructional Support Teacher for Mathematics
Grant Middle School
Syracuse, New York

The Metamorphosis of a Stellar Lecturer

Here, Gregory Russo, a high school history and geography teacher, gives us a candid account of a teacher who, according to many more traditional criteria, would be regarded as a very good instructor. Gregory's commentary supplies us with a marvelous recounting of a traditional teacher's transformation into a teacher preoccupied with students' learning. If we could replicate Gregory's experiences with a few thousand teachers, more of us might end up doing formative assessment instead of merely applauding it.

For many years, I would've described myself as a typical teacher who spent most of his time in front of the class delivering what I've always regarded as fantastically entertaining lectures. My lectures definitely generated students' interest in the social studies content I was teaching, and I used to perceive myself to be a good teacher because of these "engaging" lessons. I also used to assess primarily for the purpose of giving students grades. I almost never used the test, quiz, or assignment results to inform instructional adjustments, and students certainly never saw these grade-laden assessments as a way to self-assess their understanding. Most of the time, they would wait a week or more to find out their grade, and when they did find out their grade, their papers usually ended up in the trash a few minutes later. The main purpose of the grade was usually to validate how the students already perceived themselves as learners.

Everything I thought I knew about effective teaching changed after I attended a conference titled "Transforming Students into Learners," where the program was heavily influenced by the formative assessment work of British researchers Dylan Wiliam and Paul Black. I left the conference a bit dumbfounded, beginning to get an inkling of the vast possibilities of what truly effective teaching and learning could look like. I've since come to realize that effective teaching is not about my being the center of attention in the classroom but about making student learning the center of the classroom.

My metamorphosis first took place with students self-monitoring their progress toward the learning target each day on a worksheet that graphically tracked their progress. Students would have to reflect on their understanding of the lesson's objective at the end of the lesson by asking themselves if they got it, kind of got it, or needed help. I would then have students show a thumbs up, sideways, or down. In addition, I had students rate their level of effort for that particular class period. This small step revealed to both me and my students their understanding of the learning target. For the first time, both my students and I were using concrete data based on their level of understanding to plan out the next steps for learning.

This was a major turning point, in which students were beginning to take ownership of their learning. This was most noticeable in the classroom climate, where students were no longer receiving grades passively, but were now actively involved with their learning process. A surprise to me was that my lowest-performing students were starting to buy into the process. These students were beginning to connect their effort, reflections, and level of understanding on a particular lesson objective to their overall success in class.

Some of the practices that emerged from my use of formative assessment included giving students the unit and lesson objectives ahead of time to allow them to more accurately anticipate the direction of their learning. Another was to have students participate in data discussions before and after quizzes and tests. During these discussions, students would predict how they would perform on a quiz or test, and then, afterward, analyze their test results and plan next steps for learning based on the data. Lately, we have taken time to co-create rubrics to help describe proficiency.

If you enter my classroom today, you will most likely find me working with small groups of students as a guide helping to facilitate their learning. I spend most of my time giving immediate feedback to students about their progress. Students are in charge of the formative process, and they take full responsibility for their successes and failures. I might not be the center of attention anymore, but I am OK with that. This is because I know my students are reaching their full potential as learners.

Gregory Russo
History and World Geography Teacher
Westminster High School
Westminster, Colorado

When to Adjust, and How?

One of the most vexing questions facing teachers who use formative assessment is when to make an instructional adjustment. In essence, the issue revolves around the number of students who seem to be at sea before the teacher decides an instructional life preserver should be tossed to them. Kimberly Campbell, whom we met back on page 174, worries about this question in her science classes. She also worries about how to make the instructional adjustments that can shrink the gap between where unsuccessful students currently are and where they need to be. In this commentary, Kimberly addresses both of these issues and offers us an intriguing assessment technique for getting an en-route fix on her students' levels of understanding.

My colleagues and I embarked on the formative assessment journey as a department. Early on, the biggest question every week was, "How many students must 'not be there' to warrant reteaching something all over again?" Talking these decisions through with trusted colleagues helped. Yet, as is the case with any education technique, making it your own is the key to making it work. And, of course, just because it works one way in first period does not mean it will work the same way in later periods.

Knowing myself and my own subject (science) was the first step to finding assessments that worked for me. For example, assessments that called for students to redo their homework problems on the board would not be suitable if the homework I had assigned was opinion-based in nature. Then, I had to consider the behavior of my students. For most of the classes, using assessments based on scientific manipulatives worked very well. But I had one class in which my students were so distracted by manipulatives that they couldn't concentrate on the material we were studying.

In the end, though, comes the question of what to do once you know what students do not know. It is rare that assessment results come back indicating all students have mastered something at precisely the same level. Typically, there will be a student who needs to be pushed a little in the right direction to gain understanding. Then you have to decide how to get everyone to the same place without boring those who already have mastered something. My answer to this often turns toward having those who do understand assist others who don't.

One example of this is when we do Four Corners. With this process, you automatically know who understands and who does not. Four Corners starts with the teacher giving students a four-option multiple-choice test item. Each corner of the room is designated as one of the answer choices. Students move to the corner of the room representing what they think to be the correct answer. Then, the teacher asks each group to explain why they believe their answer to be the correct one. Students in each corner can talk this over before replying. The aim here is to let students hear one other reason through the process of arriving at their answer. As it turns out, one or two corners of the room are usually vacant—meaning nobody's chosen that answer—and in these cases, the teacher randomly calls on any student to explain why those choices were no good. I love how, with Four Corners, assessment is so clearly used in the service of learning.

Kimberly Campbell
Science Teacher
Carver High School
Winston-Salem, North Carolina

A Framework for Effective and Efficient Teaching and Learning

In this commentary, a recently retired elementary school teacher, Mary Joy Carlson, looks back at the ease with which she was able to transfer formative assessment procedures in reading to her own specialty of mathematics. Mary Joy saw immediately that the really significant aspects of formative assessment would work well whether kids were coping with Pythagorean problems or ferreting out a paragraph's main idea. As she now tries out—with college students—the formative assessment ploys she first used with elementary students, I'll bet Mary Joy will discover formative assessment works equally well with these "grown-ups."

During the past few years, we devoted hundreds of hours to improving reading instruction. We learned about setting the stage by developing background knowledge, identifying target skills, making those target skills visible to our students, and developing vocabulary. We established guided-reading groups and constantly monitored students' reading progress so that we could provide interventions based on the individual needs of our students. All of this work required deliberate planning and scheduling. Of course, the focus on reading was so intense that we neglected to apply this deliberate planning to other content areas!

When I was introduced to formative assessment in my role as an instructional support teacher for mathematics, the parallels to the reading structures already in place were quite apparent. Formative assessment's stress on sharing learning goals with students corresponds to the ways in which we were already displaying the target skills for the reading lesson. Listing success criteria parallels setting the stage for the reading selection. Planning how and when to assess learning is just like progress monitoring. And the differentiated instruction that formative assessment data can inform is similar to establishing intervention groups. For me, using formative assessment was just a logical step to provide continuity in planning, establishing instructional routines, and clearly defining expectations. Simply put, it provides a framework for effective and efficient teaching and learning.

In my formatively oriented classroom, prominently displaying the learning goals and the success criteria kept both my students and me mindful of what we were trying to achieve. The tasks were aligned to the success criteria, and students were able to monitor their own progress as they worked and assumed responsibility for their learning. They were learning to become independent and not constantly relying on me to tell them whether or not they were "getting it." Formative assessment is not about the teacher and the teaching. It is about the learner and the learning.

I retired from public school teaching at the end of the last school year, and am currently teaching a mathematics course at a local university. When I began planning my classes, I decided that I would incorporate some components of formative assessment. At the beginning of each session, I post the learning goals and success criteria for that day. I've noticed that many of the students copy these into their notes. Hopefully, they are using them as a guide for studying and reviewing. In any event, the students know exactly what they are responsible for. The need to ask, "Will this be on the test?" has been eliminated, and I have defined the questions that I will ask and assessment tasks that I will assign. I am eager to use more formative assessment techniques with my new, more mature students.

Mary Joy Carlson
Instructional Support Teacher (Retired)
McKinley-Brighton Elementary School
Syracuse, New York

The Missing Piece—Puzzle Solved!

Puzzle-people love to arrive at solutions—it's so satisfying! In this next commentary, we hear from a high school science teacher, D'Lane Joens, who found that formative assessment was the answer to her very own instructional puzzle. She makes assessment-gathered evidence a pivotal part of her instructional decision making, as well as a key element in the learning-related choices of her students. Here's a teacher who truly is using formative assessment the way it is supposed to be used.

For me, as an educator, formative assessment was like finding the missing piece of the puzzle! Before being exposed to formative assessment, I had been refining the essential learning targets for my classes and working on getting students to chart their own progress. Still, my instruction often felt like I was "going through the motions." Each day, the focus was on my doing and not on students' learning. When I encountered formative assessment, I finally understood what had been the missing piece in my instruction.

After using formative assessment in my classroom for a year, I am hooked—and so are my high school science students. It is easy, it makes learning meaningful for my students, and it has provided me with the necessary information to help each student help him- or herself! Many of the assessments I employ as part of the formative assessment process are techniques I have used for years, and, after a little more research, I have found an abundance of science-related assessments I can use for this purpose. I incorporate them into my daily planning, with most of the assessments taking two to five minutes. Because I was told not to grade formative assessments, my workload has decreased. To alleviate the overuse of paper and to smooth transitions, I have a pencil box with scrap paper, colored pencils, and markers on each group's table. Almost all assessments are done on this paper. It's quick and it's easy!

After I carefully explain the purpose of an assessment that I'm using formatively, my students never ask me to grade them. They understand and accept that formative assessment is in place to help them understand what they know and don't know. My students self-assess and immediately document their growth and any problems they are encountering on their progress-monitoring sheets. Students understand that this is a daily part of their learning. It provides them with concrete information that they can use to change their learning tactics and to reach their desired learning targets. To assist them with changing their learning tactics, I have carved out a small portion of time each week when the students can work on their problem areas, ask questions, or push themselves beyond the required proficiency. For the most part, students really enjoy this time because *they* are in control of their learning, not me.

The information I get from these assessments helps me tweak my lessons for immediate results. This doesn't take as much time as I had originally thought it would. Usually an instructional adjustment involves a quick reteach or working with a small group of students who don't understand. Students appreciate this because I don't drag the entire class through another lesson unless the formative assessment evidence says it's necessary.

Using the formative assessment process has given my students' learning real meaning and, at the same time, it has truly transformed my teaching.

D'Lane Joens
Science Department Chairperson
Platte Valley High School
Kersey, Colorado

Reflection Questions

1. The educators who contributed the commentaries in this chapter live in various parts of the United States and learned about formative assessment from a variety of sources. What similarities and differences do you see in the way they think about and apply formative assessment? Do you see the differences as major or minor? Can you identify any perceptions about formative assessment that appear to be universal?

2. Which of the chapter's commentaries do you think made the most persuasive case for formative assessment? Why?

3. Which of the specific formative assessment techniques cited in this chapter do you think would be a good fit for your classroom and your students? Why?

Conclusion

In education, anything that can become overcomplicated almost always will be, and formative assessment is not immune to this indictment. In the preceding pages, we have looked at the formative assessment process dissected into different applications—five ways to use it. If you've read *TA1*, you know that it can also be carved into different levels; we're talking about the same thing, just talking about it in different ways.

You've seen that formative assessment can be used by teachers and can also be used by students. Moreover, you've seen that the assessment evidence that's so central to this process can be collected in many, many ways. Yes, *conceptually*, formative assessment can easily become overwhelmingly complex. *But it doesn't need to be.*

In its most unadorned incarnation, formative assessment simply calls for teachers or students to employ assessment-elicited evidence to do better whatever they've been doing. When teachers set out to install some version of formative assessment, they always need to collect assessment *evidence* from students. This is because, in formative assessment, the adequacy of a teacher's instruction or a student's learning tactic is determined neither by intuition nor whim, but by data. The quality of whatever is going on is always judged *primarily* according to its impact on students' learning.

One Process, Five Applications

In the previous pages, you've learned about five ways the formative assessment process can be employed. You have read, in turn, about teachers using formative assessment to make immediate adjustments, near-future adjustments, and last-chance adjustments in their ongoing instruction. You've seen that formative assessment can be employed by students to determine whether to adjust their current learning tactics. Finally, you saw how the combination of a teacher's instructional adjustments and students' learning tactic adjustments can, if the teacher sets out to do so, bring about a fundamental shift in the climate of a classroom.

In all five applications, teachers will face a set of choices that, if made astutely, will make formative assessment a rousing success for their students. Learning progressions come in because this process needs to be thoughtfully planned. Monitoring students' mastery of a learning progression leads to evidence collection for each building block in a progression. And, as I stressed throughout the book, because of current research evidence supporting formative assessment's robustness, there are no sacrosanct commandments about how the formative assessment process must be implemented—other than to collect assessment evidence as the basis for adjustment decisions. There are many ways to play the formative assessment game and, happily, almost all of them turn out to be good for students. And if educators can understand the key components of the formative assessment process, then the applications of formative assessment, such as the ones you have read about in this book, can be pulled off with ease and aplomb and with infinite variation.

In Chapter 9, you saw real comments from actual teachers in the field, testifying to the value they've found in formative assessment. And you've read accounts of amalgam, fictional teachers planning and implementing formative assessment—and explaining the kinds of choices they make. The mission of those interviews was to illustrate the kind of thinking that's required from a teacher who wants to make formative assessment work well—not the one and only way to do it, because there isn't one and only way, but examples of the *sort of thinking* that's needed when one decides to hop into the deep end of the formative assessment pool.

What's Next?

I wrote this book for one simple reason: I believed that if I could demystify the nature of the formative assessment process, additional teachers might be willing to give it a try. But, whether you are currently a teacher who might begin using formative assessment yourself or a school leader who might encourage others to use formative assessment, the next move is up to you.

One way you can dip your toe into the formative assessment wading pool is to carve out a tiny chunk of one of the applications of formative assessment and give it a try in your own setting. If you're a teacher, try something teensy in your own class. If you're a school-site administrator, encourage one or more teachers in your school to experiment a bit with just a modest element of what you've been reading about in these pages. The easiest thing to do when reading a book such as this is to understand what its message is, and even to agree with that message, but then set it aside because other tasks are beckoning. But a set-aside book changes nothing. The children with whom you work won't benefit from a set-aside book. What's needed from you now is *action*.

A Close-Out "Thought Experiment"

I don't know about you, but I always become instantly engaged when I'm in an audience and have been told by a presenter that, in the next few moments, we'll all take part in a thought experiment. To me, "a thought experiment" sounds intrinsically exotic.

And so I want to conclude this book by asking you, *right this minute*, to participate in a two-part thought experiment. I'm hoping it will illustrate why those of us who have any influence over what goes on in our schools should valiantly endeavor to get formative assessment used in more classrooms. You can think of it as an experiment in comparative anger allocation.

Part I: A Medical Scenario

Please imagine that a virulent new strain of chicken pox has surfaced in many parts of the nation. Children from ages 6 to 12 are particularly susceptible to this disease that, though not life-threatening, requires any infected youngster to be quarantined at home for a minimum of five weeks.

Imagine, further, that the nation's pharmaceutical industry has discovered a low-cost, research-proven vaccine to prevent children from becoming infected with the new chicken pox strain—a vaccine with no side effects. However, physicians, and particularly pediatricians, do almost nothing to (1) urge their medical colleagues to administer the vaccine or (2) inform parents about the vaccine's preventative virtues. Because of this inaction by medical professionals, many children become infected and are quarantined at home for five weeks or more.

Here's where the thought experiment kicks in. Imagine that you are a parent of one of these quarantined youngsters. You not only see that your child is missing out on many weeks of school, but you must provide the child-care support that a child with chicken pox requires. Now, given this situation, how angry would you be toward the medical professionals who failed to actively advocate use of the new chickenpox vaccine? On a scale of 1 to 10, with 10 being the most angry, *how angry would you be* with the unassertive medical professionals whose inaction led to your child's illness?

Part II: An Educational Scenario

Switching venues, imagine now that educational researchers have discovered a low-cost, research-proven process capable of dramatically improving children's learning. Yet educational professionals (1) do not seriously attempt to bring this powerful process to the attention of the nation's educators or (2) try to make parents of school-age children aware of its effectiveness. Because of this inactivity, literally *thousands* of children receive a far less effective education than they could have received.

Again, please imagine that you are a parent of one of these inadequately educated children, a child who could have accomplished so much more with a more effective education. Once more, *how angry would you be*—on a scale of 1 to 10—with the educators whose inaction reduced the quality of education your child received?

Because this is a thought experiment, I don't know how your two numerical anger-estimates compare. But I do know that in the medical scenario, the adverse consequences could be counted in weeks, while in the educational scenario, the adverse effects involved are potentially lifelong.

To wrap up this anger-allocation experiment, then, please consider the following short-answer completion question:

> Educators who know about the profound positive impact formative assessment has on children's learning, yet fail to aggressively advocate its adoption, should be characterized as _____.

You can fill in the blank.

References

Arter, J. A. (2010). *Interim benchmark assessments: Are we getting our eggs in the right basket?* Paper presented at the annual conference of the National Council on Measurement in Education, Denver, CO, May 1, 2010.

Black, P., & Wiliam, D. (1998). Assessment and classroom learning. *Assessment in Education: Principles, Policy and Practice, 5*(1), 7–73.

Cooper, A., & Jenson, G. (2009). Practical processes for teaching habits of mind. In A. L. Costa and B. Kallick (Eds.), *Habits of mind across the curriculum: Practical and creative strategies for teachers* (pp. 17–35). Alexandria, VA: ASCD.

Erwin, J. C. (2010). *Inspiring the best in students.* Alexandria, VA: ASCD.

Heritage, M. (2008, July). *Learning progressions: Supporting instruction and formative assessment.* Paper prepared for the Formative Assessment for Teachers and Students (FAST) State Collaborative on Assessment and Student Standards (SCASS) of the Council of Chief State School Officers (CCSSO). Available: http://www.ccsso.org/Resources/Publications/Learning_Progressions_Supporting_Instruction_and_Formative_Assessment.html

Heritage, M. H. (2010). *Formative assessment: Making it happen in the classroom.* Thousand Oaks, CA: Corwin Press.

Heritage, M., Kim, J., Vendlinski, T., & Herman, J. (2009). From evidence to action: A seamless process in formative assessment? *Educational Measurement: Issues and Practice, 28*(3), 24–31.

Pellegrino, J. W., & Goldman, S. R. (2007). Beyond rhetoric: Realities and complexities of integrating assessment into teaching and learning. In C. Dwyer (Ed.) *The future of assessment: Shaping teaching and learning* (pp. 7–52). Mahwah, NJ: Erlbaum.

Popham, W. J. (2008). *Transformative assessment.* Alexandria, VA: ASCD.

Popham, W. J. (2011). *Classroom assessment: What teachers need to know* (6th ed.). Boston: Pearson.

Stiggins, R. J. (2006). *An introduction to student-involved assessment for learning* (5th ed.). Boston: Pearson.

Sullo, B. (2009). *The motivated student: Unlocking the enthusiasm for learning.* Alexandria, VA: ASCD.

Index

The letter *f* following a page number denotes a figure.

About the Author

W. James Popham is Emeritus Professor in the UCLA Graduate School of Education and Information Studies. He has spent most of career as a teacher, largely at UCLA, where for nearly 30 years he taught courses in instructional methods for prospective teachers and graduate-level courses in evaluation and measurement. At UCLA he won several distinguished teaching awards, and in January 2000, he was recognized by *UCLA Today* as one of UCLA's top 20 professors of the 20th century.

In 1968, Dr. Popham established IOX Assessment Associates, a research and development group that created statewide student achievement tests for a dozen states. In 2002, the National Council on Measurement in Education presented him with its Award for Career Contributions to Educational Measurement. He is a former president of the American Educational Research Association (AERA) and the founding editor of *Educational Evaluation and Policy Analysis,* an AERA quarterly journal. In 2006, he was awarded a Certificate of Recognition by the National Association of Test Directors. In October 2009, he was appointed by Secretary of Education Arne Duncan to the National Assessment Governing Board, the policy-setting group for the National Assessment of Educational Progress.

Dr. Popham is the author of more than 30 books, 200 journal articles, 50 research reports, and nearly 200 papers presented before research societies. His most recent books are *Classroom Assessment: What Teachers Need to Know*, 6th edition (2011); *Unlearned Lessons: Six Stumbling Blocks to Our Schools' Success* (2009); *Instruction That Measures Up: Successful Teaching in the Age of Accountability* (2009), *Transformative Assessment* (2008); *Assessment for Educational Leaders* (2006); *Mastering Assessment: A Self-Service System for Educators* (2006); *America's "Failing" Schools: How Parents and Teachers Can Cope with No Child Left Behind* (2005); *Test Better, Teach Better: The Instructional Role of Assessment* (2003); and *The Truth About Testing: An Educator's Call to Action* (2001).

Related ASCD Resources: Formative Assessment

At the time of publication, the following ASCD resources were available (ASCD stock numbers appear in parentheses). For up-to-date information about ASCD resources, go to www.ascd.org. You can search the complete archives of *Educational Leadership* at http://www.ascd.org/el.

ASCD Edge
Exchange ideas and connect with other educators interested in assessment on the social networking site ASCD Edge™ at http://ascdedge.ascd.org/

Multimedia
Formative Assessment Strategies for Every Classroom (2nd ed.): An ASCD Action Tool by Susan M. Brookhart (#111005)

Online Professional Development
Formative Assessment: The Basics (#PD09OC69). Visit the ASCD website (www.ascd.org).

Print Products
Advancing Formative Assessment in Every Classroom: A Guide for Instructional Leaders by Connie M. Moss and Susan M. Brookhart (#109031)

Checking for Understanding: Formative Assessment Techniques for Your Classroom by Douglas Fisher and Nancy Frey (#107023)

Exploring Formative Assessment (The Professional Learning Community Series) by Susan M. Brookhart (#109038)

Transformative Assessment by W. James Popham (#108018)

What Teachers Really Need to Know About Formative Assessment by Laura Greenstein (#110017)

Videos
Formative Assessment in Content Areas (series of three 25-minute DVDs, each with a professional development program) (#609034)

The Power of Formative Assessment to Advance Learning (series of three 25- to 30-minute DVDs, with a comprehensive user guide) (#608066)

For more information: send e-mail to member@ascd.org; call 1-800-933-2723 or 703-578-9600, press 2; send a fax to 703-575-5400; or write to Information Services, ASCD, 1703 N. Beauregard St., Alexandria, VA 22311-1714 USA.